501
UNARMED
SELF-DEFENSE SKILLS

501
UNARMED
SELF-DEFENSE SKILLS

CHRIS McNAB

THUNDER BAY
P · R · E · S · S
San Diego, California

Thunder Bay Press
An imprint of Printers Row Publishing Group
10350 Barnes Canyon Road, Suite 100, San Diego, CA 92121
www.thunderbaybooks.com

Thunder Bay Press
Publisher: Peter Norton
Publishing Team: Lori Asbury, Ana Parker, Kathryn Chipinka, Aaron Guzman
Editorial Team: JoAnn Padgett, Melinda Allman, Dan Mansfield

Editorial and design by
Amber Books Ltd, 74–77 White Lion Street, London, N1 9PF, United Kingdom
www.amberbooks.co.uk

Project Editor: Michael Spilling
Design: Brian Rust
Illustrations: Tony Randell

Library of Congress Cataloging-in-Publication Data

Names: McNab, Chris, 1970- author.
Title: 501 unarmed self-defense skills / Chris McNab.
Description: San Diego, California : Thunder Bay Press, [2017] | Includes index.
Identifiers: LCCN 2016037318 | ISBN 9781626868458
Subjects: LCSH: Self-defense.
Classification: LCC GV1111 .A14 2017 | DDC 613.6/6--dc23
LC record available at https://lccn.loc.gov/2016037318

Printed in China

20 19 18 17 16   1 2 3 4 5

Contents

INTRODUCTION

Self-defense is one of those subjects plagued by myths. The greatest myth, largely propagated by action movies, is that of invincibility. Here the well-trained warrior always wins through a mixture of superlative technique and unwavering courage. His celluloid battles are brutally but beautifully choreographed, with astonishing and complex moves, and he ultimately defeats all challengers.

In reality, no matter how expert a person becomes in unarmed combat, he will always remain terribly vulnerable in a street fight. Ask anyone who regularly faces true violence, such as nightclub doormen or police officers, and almost all will confess to feeling deep fear before and during any fight. This fear comes from knowing that a person can go from victor to vanquished in the space of a single opportunistic punch. Real fights, unlike those in the movies, always have uncertain outcomes.

The second myth is slightly more insidious, as it can be propagated even among those who have achieved a high level in the martial arts. This is the belief that somehow fights can be clean and controlled, and that knowing advanced techniques can guarantee victory. I have a friend who has never done a day's martial arts training in his life, but instead has fought (and won) hundreds of real clashes as a nightclub bouncer. He says that he can always identify trained martial artists, because in the immediate prefight buildup they often start bouncing on the spot, as if in a competition fight. Invariably, so my trusted friend observes, such people are easy to beat, because they are not generally accustomed to the brutal and painful close-quarters chaos of a real fight. The core lesson here is that actual fights are "messy," and do not conform to the highly regimented fight routines of martial arts training. They also involve an explosion of adrenaline that can paralyze even the most well-studied fighter, if he has not experienced this in earnest before.

This book brings together a collection of 501 self-defense tips, from all fighting disciplines. These techniques and attitudes, if practiced until they become second nature, will absolutely improve your chances of survival in a street fight, if they are implemented with a ferocious fighting spirit. But there is no glory in physically damaging another human being because you can, nor is there any value in saving face if it results in your hospitalization or death. Hence the underlying and emphatic message of this book is to use all your wit, guile, and self-preservation to avoid fights in the first place. This is the true path of self-defense, and the mark of a humble and compassionate human being.

1. FITNESS REGIME

To train your body for combat, implement a fitness regime with equal focus on strength and stamina training. The former provides power, while the latter provides endurance.

2. HIGH AND LOW

When weight training, do a mixture of high weights/ low reps and low weights/high reps. Focusing only on heavy weights can result in a loss of speed when punching and kicking.

3. "SEVENS"

For arm and shoulder development, try "sevens"— seven push-ups from full-arm lockdown to the midpoint and back, seven from the ground position to midpoint and back, and then seven full push-ups. Do this set three times.

4. HILL RUNNING

Instead of flat-surface running, try hill running. The uneven surface and changes in gradient will force you to adjust your pace, stride, and tempo.

5. REST AND RECOVERY

Remember to include at least one day of total rest in your weekly exercise program to allow for complete muscle recovery and body rejuvenation.

6. EXPLOSIVE POWER

Combat involves explosive actions. Try sports in which the legwork mirrors this kind of action. Good examples are badminton, tennis, volleyball, and sprinting for 100 yards.

7. CORE STRENGTH

Strong core muscles are imperative for powerful punching and fast legwork. You can build up abdominal muscles with crunches, leg raises, and kettlebell pullovers.

8. PROTEIN LOADING

To aid muscle development, load up on high-quality proteins, such as lean meats, and make sure that these foods are grilled rather than fried to avoid excessive calories.

9. HIP STRENGTH

Develop your hip flexibility for effective kicking and knee work by adopting a deep, wide leg squat and using your elbows to gently but firmly push your knees wider apart.

10. PROPER HYDRATION

Make sure that you stay properly hydrated before, during, and after exercise. Your urine will be very light in color when you are fully hydrated, and dark if you are dehydrated.

11. CIRCUIT TRAINING

Circuit training is an ideal form of rounded body exercise for combat training. There should be at least 30 seconds of rest between each individual circuit, to allow the heart rate to recover.

12. KEEPING FORM

During weight training, always ensure that you keep good form throughout the exercises. Keeping form is more important than trying to push the number of reps until you feel muscle failure.

13. PUNCH BAG

A workout with a punch bag or focus pad is one of the best ways to improve your fighting stamina. Go full-out against the pad for 30 seconds, rest for 15 seconds, and then repeat this pattern two more times. Build up until you are continually punching for a full minute.

14. EXTRA EXERCISES

Increase your level of activity outside the gym to build up your stamina and burn off extra calories. Good examples of extra exercises include dancing, gardening, DIY projects, and simply standing instead of sitting.

15. DUMBBELL SQUATS

Hold a dumbbell against your chest and do repeated low-leg squats. This exercise will build up strength in your thighs and gluteus muscles, giving you greater power in leg movements.

16. PLANK

The plank is a useful exercise for building up core muscle strength and control. Ensure that you adopt the correct position, with your back, buttocks, and legs in alignment.

17. PLANK (VARIATION)

On a shiny, slippery floor, you can increase the impact of your plank by putting a towel under each foot and then pulling yourself backward and forward a few inches, using your elbows.

18. STRETCHING TECHNIQUE

When performing a stretch, take it to its maximum extent and then relax into it for a few moments, allowing the muscles to elongate. Take a deep breath, and as you breathe out, lean into the stretch.

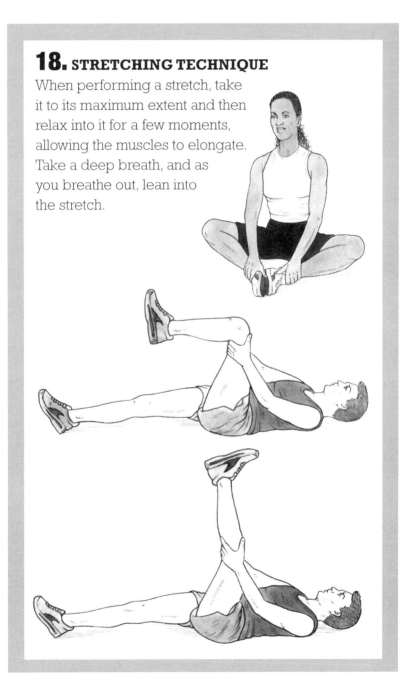

19. FLEXIBILITY TRAINING

Don't neglect flexibility. Devote one hour each week to flexibility training, particularly focusing on your hips and on your core and shoulders.

20. MEDICINE BALL

A medicine ball is a traditional and highly effective tool for developing muscular speed and strength. For example, performing a sit-up with a medicine ball and passing it to a partner at the top of the sit-up is a good core exercise.

21. PUSH-UPS

When doing conventional push-ups, place your hands shoulder-width apart, and as you move upward or downward, keep the elbows tucked in, brushing the sides of the body as you ascend and descend.

22. PUSH-UPS (VARIATION)

A variation on the push-up position is to place your hands on the floor with the fingers pointing inward, so that your elbows bend outward as you go down. This helps develop the biceps and triceps as well as the shoulder muscles.

23. CRASH DIET

If you are trying to lose weight, avoid extreme low-calorie crash diets. Weight loss is more sustainable in the long term if caloric intake is significantly reduced but remains high enough to meet energy needs.

24. GOOD DIET

Ensure that you implement a proper diet to support your training regime. Avoid foods that are high in saturated fat and sugar, and instead opt for lean proteins, carbohydrates, and plenty of fruit and vegetables.

25. CARB BOOST

Eating a large carbohydrate meal, such as a bowl of pasta, about two hours before exercising will give you an energy boost during training.

26. MIX IT UP

When weight training, mix your exercises between the free weights and weight machines. Weight machines allow you to lift heavier weights without a spotter, but free weights produce more rounded muscular development.

27. HAMSTRING STRETCH

To keep your hamstrings loose and flexible, sit on the floor with your legs stretched out. Slide your hands slowly down your legs, but keep your head up and face forward, to avoid hunching your back.

28. SHADOWBOXING

To quicken the speed of your punches, do some shadowboxing while holding light (3–10 pounds) grip weights. Make sure that you fully extend your punches during this exercise.

29. INTERVAL TRAINING

When running, build a form of interval training into the route. Do slow jogging between some points interspersed with fast sprinting between other points. This will increase your energy and help develop explosive speed.

30. BREATHE DEEPLY

When performing any stretch, breathe regularly and deeply throughout the exercise to keep your muscles properly oxygenated.

31. PATIENT RECOVERY

When recovering from muscular injuries, don't attempt to rush the healing process. Patiently work the injured muscle through range-of-movement and extension exercises, stopping if you experience any pain.

32. IRREGULAR MOVEMENTS

Attempt some forms of exercise that contain a high degree of irregular movements. Moving heavy objects, such as plant pots or breeze blocks, over uneven terrain is a good example.

33. SWIMMING

For all-around body development, swimming is one of the best forms of exercise. Vary the types of strokes you use in order to give different muscle groups a workout.

34. ADRENALINE RUSH

In a fight situation, fear releases adrenaline into the blood system, providing a surge of energy to the muscles. It is critical that you psychologically manage the energy release, or it can result in mental and physical paralysis.

35. FEAR RESPONSE

Symptoms of the adrenal reaction include physical shaking, a trembling voice, sweating, a dry mouth, feelings of nausea, a loss of bowel or bladder control, tunnel vision, and time-perception distortions.

36. "I CAN HANDLE HIM."

One way to counter fear is to contradict each negative thought that pops into your head with a positive one. For example, instead of thinking, "He is much bigger than I am," say, "I can handle him."

37. BREATHE FOR CONTROL

In the buildup to a confrontation, keep breathing deeply and smoothly. It will help you command your mental processes as well as control your anxiety to a certain degree.

38. TWITCH YOUR TOES

Channel your fear into movement to give the adrenaline some release. In a prefight phase, this can be as simple as twitching your toes in your shoes or clenching and unclenching your fists.

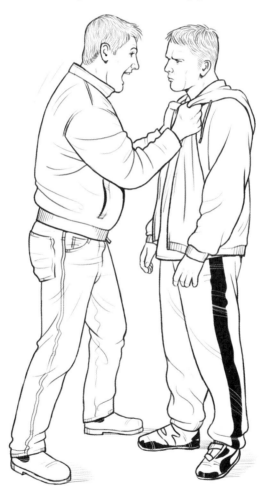

39. STAY IN THE MOMENT

Don't mentally predict a negative outcome to the fight. Instead, focus entirely upon your actions and the techniques of survival.

40. UNLEASH YOUR AGGRESSION

If a confrontation turns dangerous and poses a genuine threat to your well-being, completely unleash your aggression. A ferocious attitude and an absolute commitment to the fight will often compensate for inadequacies of technique.

41. VISUALIZATION TECHNIQUES

Use visualization techniques to supplement your physical training. Imagine, as vividly as you can, various fight scenarios. Picture yourself handling the situations with confidence and focused aggression.

42. VISUALIZATION 1

To begin the process of visualization, find a quiet place to sit or lie down, where you will be undisturbed for about 15 minutes.

43. VISUALIZATION 2

Sitting or lying comfortably, focus on the rise and fall of your breathing. With every breath that goes out, feel all the muscles in your body soften and relax.

44. VISUALIZATION 3

Next, relax each muscle in your body, from your toes to your scalp. Tense each muscle in turn, and then release the tension and allow the muscle to relax to its fullest extent.

45. VISUALIZATION 4

As you relax the muscles of your body, keep slowing your breathing and internally saying, "Relax . . ." Once you are fully relaxed, you can begin visualization.

46. VISUALIZATION 5

Picture an intimidating assailant coming toward you with aggressive intent. Imagine the scene very vividly, including its sounds, colors, and smells as well as the sensations in your body.

47. VISUALIZATION 6

Now, picture yourself responding in the way that you would want to respond. This doesn't necessarily mean an act of violence. You might imagine talking to the assailant and defusing the situation.

48. VISUALIZATION 7

If you picture the situation as a fight, don't imagine fantastical martial arts moves. "See" yourself as a ferocious fighter, using simple, powerful fighting techniques that come naturally and easily.

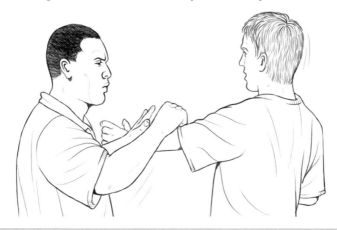

49. VISUALIZATION 8

After you have mentally rehearsed the situation several times, with different threats and developments, slowly count backward from five to one, and on "one" open your eyes and come out of the visualization session.

50. STOCK YOUR MEMORY

Visualization works by stocking your memory with preexisting mental models of combat, decreasing the chances of your freezing during an actual encounter.

51. FACE YOUR FEARS

Make confidence and mental strength part of your everyday life, not just your unarmed combat training. Make it a habit to confront situations that you find uncomfortable or challenging.

52. BUT BE CAREFUL...

As a counterbalance to Tip 51, don't overestimate your abilities and seek out trouble. Violence always has uncertain outcomes, and violent acts should be avoided at all costs.

53. MENTALLY PREPARE

When you meet a new person, mentally rehearse what it would involve to fight that person. Become acclimatized to having physical confidence in the presence of many different types of people.

54. RELEASE YOUR INNER TIGER

In a confrontation, imagine yourself as a wild animal, fighting with completely unconscious ferocity and a commitment to survival.

55. KATA

Learn the *kata*, the fixed sequences of movements associated with a martial art. Practice the movements with a martial spirit, mentally picturing your success as you tackle multiple opponents.

56. SCREAM!

Releasing a formidable scream during an attack—known in karate as a *ki-ai*—can help you overcome the fear of combat and give you greater focus and power in your techniques.

57. FIND YOUR BALANCE

Practice balance techniques, such as standing on one leg and reaching down to pick up objects without falling over. These exercises help with the balance needed for kicking, and they improve concentration and focus.

58. MOVE AWAY

Be ultra alert regarding people and surroundings when you are in a potentially threatening environment. The simplest survival technique is to move away from trouble in its incipient stages.

59. WATCH FOR SIGNS

Train yourself to be fully aware of some of the classic body language signs of impending violence. Many fights begin with little more than aggressive eye contact.

60. ESCALATION

As an aggressor escalates toward an attack, he will typically display intimidating body language, such as arm splaying, a pecking head action, and wide eyes. When observing such signs, prepare to defend yourself.

61. IMMINENT THREAT

An attacker's body language may be accentuated with harsh, short statements or questions. The speech of an attacker is typically punctuated with expletives. Immediately prior to striking, his verbal language may devolve into single syllables as he controls his breathing to prepare for the attack.

62. HIT FIRST

If all the signs indicate that you are about to be attacked, be first to go into action. Keep in mind the following axiom: "Hit first, hit hard, keep hitting."

63. CRACK A JOKE

In the buildup to a potentially aggressive confrontation, try to give the hostile party some way out of fighting. Properly judged humor can defuse a number of hostile situations.

64. PARK YOUR EGO

Don't let your ego stop you from backing down from a fight. Engage in physical violence only if you are unavoidably and directly threatened with a vicious attack.

65. STAY STRONG

Although you should do all you can to defuse rising tension, do not act weak, because this may inspire the aggressor to think that you are a soft target. Keep your body language upright and strong, and your voice confident.

66. AVOID DISTRACTIONS

If approached by strange people with apparently innocent questions, be aware of what is happening all around you, as they could be distracting you for an attacker.

67. WATCH THEIR HANDS

When you have identified suspicious persons, closely watch their hands to check for weapons. Be particularly wary if they constantly dip their hands in and out of their pockets.

68. BE SAFE

Self-defense begins with an awareness of your surroundings. Avoid any areas that are known for violence. If you're in a strange city, ask local people or police to identify those places for you on a map.

69. WATCH THE WATCHERS

Be careful if approached by people exhibiting erratic eye movements, as they might be evaluating the surroundings to see if there is an opportunity to strike.

70. BE AWARE OF SETUPS

Be watchful for attackers who try to set you up using distracting gestures. These acts or movements can be as simple as asking for the time or for directions somewhere. Don't take your eyes off their bodies and their hands.

71. LOCK YOUR CAR

One very simple protective measure is to always lock your car the moment you get inside it. Do this before you do anything else, such as putting on a seat belt.

72. GO MAD

If cornered by a highly aggressive person, one option is to feign insanity. Scream wildly, let spit dribble from your mouth, and act as if insane. It could be enough to dissuade an attack.

73. TOTAL COMMITMENT

If you are attacked, don't rely on mercy or pity from your attacker. Instead, fight back with every ounce of commitment and physical strength, even if injured.

74. FOCUSED FIGHT

Remember that in a fight you are aiming either to force pain compliance or to incapacitate the attacker. Don't hit or kick without purpose or without the intent to inflict damage.

75. WATCH HIS FEET

When evaluating a potential attacker, closely study his footwork. The direction in which his feet are pointing indicates the direction he wants to go, which might be straight toward you.

76. MAKE IT UNCOMFORTABLE

If you know something about an attacker's skills, try to pitch the fight outside his comfort zone. If possible, grapple with someone who likes to fight with fists, and punch someone who prefers grappling.

77. SEIZE THE INITIATIVE

Don't be a purely defensive fighter. If you are only on the defensive, you allow the attacker to dictate the terms of the engagement. Look for and seize all opportunities to go on the offensive.

78. DRINK AND DRUGS

Study your attacker for signs of drug or alcohol consumption. Intoxication will limit the assailant's response to pain stimuli, so you might have to use more incapacitating techniques.

79. STREET FIGHTING

Most street fights follow a classic pattern: a period of aggressive posturing and fight buildup; a short, intense exchange of blows as the fighting distance closes; grappling; and then groundwork.

80. MIXED DISCIPLINES

Ensure that you can deploy a range of fighting measures. Study the impact of various kicking distances, punching ranges, and grappling measures.

81. MARTIAL ARTS

If you practice the martial arts, remember that each particular art has its own set of strengths and weaknesses. Karate, for example, is excellent for kicking and punching, but less effective for grappling.

82. HYBRID TECHNIQUES

There are some hybrid martial arts that usefully combine fighting techniques. Good examples include jujitsu and the Israeli military's Krav Maga.

83. SPARRING

The way you train in the martial arts is critical. Sparring blows against an opponent should be delivered with power and focus. Make it the opponent's responsibility—not yours—to block or avoid blows.

84. FULL CONTACT

Whatever martial art you practice, ensure that you get some full-contact fighting experience. Work on full-contact fighting is the only way to expose the flaws or limits in your techniques.

85. "ADRENALINE DUMP"

Full-contact fighting also prepares you for the "adrenaline dump" of a real fight and makes you better able to continue to fight through pain and fear.

86. PARTNER ROUTINES

When practicing partner routines, try to avoid making your efforts too choreographed and risk-free, as gentle encounters will not adequately prepare you for a real fight.

87. KEEP IT SIMPLE

It is far better to learn a few simple but powerful techniques, so they become second nature, than to acquire many complicated moves that are difficult to implement.

88. EFFECTIVE FOOTWORK

Don't focus only on learning to punch, kick, and grapple. Acquire the core skills of effective footwork, so that you can retain your balance while quickly moving into advantageous positions.

89. CORRECT CLOTHING

Think about what you wear. Make sure the fighting techniques you learn in class actually work when you are wearing your daily footwear and regular clothing.

90. FIRST AID

Learn some basic techniques of first aid. In a hard fight, it is almost certain that someone will be significantly injured, so be prepared to treat injuries.

91. PRACTICE POWER

Develop genuine power in your techniques. Any strike or kick has to have an effect on potential attackers, including people who are far larger and stronger than you are.

92. REMEMBER RESTRAINT

Don't prosecute an attack with truly disproportionate force. If someone just shoves you and walks away, don't launch into that person with potentially life-threatening blows.

93. AVOID THE FIGHT—IF YOU CAN

One rule above all else: Avoid fighting in the first place, using any means of avoidance at your disposal. Even the best martial artist cannot predict the outcome of a fight.

94. BE REALISTIC

Don't overestimate your own power. Techniques that seem decisive in the dojo can, in street fights against motivated or intoxicated opponents, appear to have little effect.

95. FIGHT TO THE END

If you fight, don't stop fighting unless your opponent is incapacitated, he convincingly submits, or you can comfortably escape. Make sure that your opponent is truly out of the fight before backing away.

96. TURN AND FIGHT

If you run from an opponent, listen for his footsteps. If he runs after you and is catching up, turn and fight. You don't want to be grabbed from behind.

97. KNOCKOUT BLOW

If you deliver a knockout blow to your opponent, try at least to be aware of how he falls to the ground. Try to prevent his striking the back of his head on the floor, as this can result in a fatal injury.

98. BREATHE OUT

When you deliver any attacking technique, breathe out sharply at the moment of impact. This action helps you tense your muscles, making your body a more solid platform for the attack.

99. PICK YOUR SPOT

Your punches, kicks, grappling techniques, and other moves should be aimed at vulnerable parts of your opponent's body. Those are the parts that are highly susceptible to pain and damage. Targeting those can force compliance.

100. HARD AND SOFT

As a broad rule, you should strike soft parts of your opponent's body with hard parts of your body, and vice versa.

101. HARD TARGET

Unless you can deliver an extremely powerful blow, or have a weapon, avoid attacking the parts of the body that are heavily protected by large muscle groups or bone. The skull and the shoulder muscles are prime examples.

102. CHOOSE EASY HITS

In a fight, the vulnerable areas of the body will not be static. Your target is likely to be moving quickly. Go for the parts that can be most conveniently accessed.

103. TARGET FOR EFFECT

Remember that the implications of attacks on each area of the body differ. A punch on the nose will produce a stinging pain, while a strike to the throat can cause suffocation and death. Target appropriately.

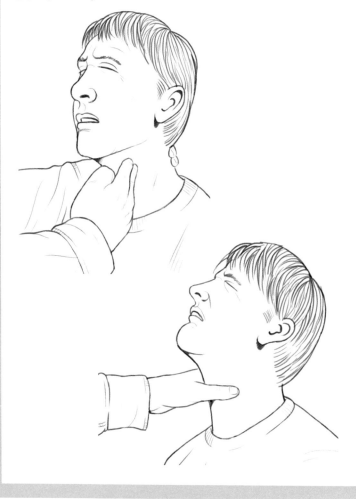

104. FOOT STOMP

Toes and the bones of the upper foot can be broken or crushed by stomping on them, although the strength of the footwear can limit the results of this method of attack.

105. SHIN SCRAPE

The shin produces intense pain if struck by a kick or scraped by the side of a shoe. Striking here can distract your opponent and set him up for another blow.

106. KNEE JOINTS

The knees are often regarded as a prime lower-limb target. However, the knee joints are difficult to target during fast-moving encounters, and they have substantial surrounding muscle protection.

107. KNEE KICK

If you are going to attack the knee, a swift kick is your best option, but don't rely on that for decisive results. Make it part of a series of other attacks.

108. GROIN TARGET

The testicles are guarded by the fighter's fast, instinctive reflex to pull back when they are threatened as well as the large thigh muscle groups on either side, so they are not an easy target.

109. DISABLING STRIKE

In men, the testicles are a natural point of attack. If struck by a kick, a punch, or a knee, they can produce a truly disabling pain and sickness, which can drop a man to his knees.

110. ABDOMEN HIT

The effect of a heavy punch or kick to the abdomen depends on several factors, such as the muscle development of the opponent. Punches here tend to be best kept as setups for more decisive attacks.

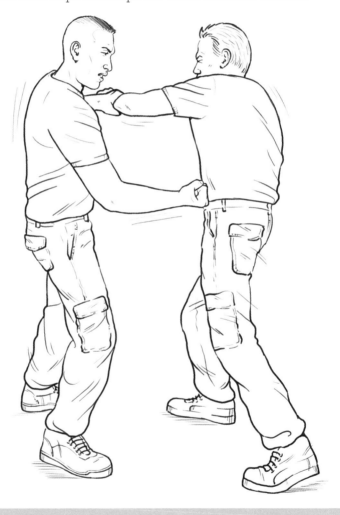

111. CLOTHING CONSIDERATIONS

Thick clothing is another protective factor for the testicles, which often prevents these organs from being grabbed. In essence, you should attack the testicles only if you have a clear and open shot.

112. DEAD LEG

The thighs can be deadened by heavy blows, and this can help slow your opponent's movements. Achieving this effect is difficult, however, especially in someone with well-developed musculature.

113. RIB CAGE

The rib cage is a strong protective cover for the torso's vital organs. Very powerful blows can break ribs, especially the "floating" ribs at the bottom of the rib cage. However, that might not be enough to stop the attacker.

114. SOLAR PLEXUS

The solar plexus is definitely a vulnerable part of the body, but it can be difficult to land a clean hit, especially if your opponent's body is turned sideways.

115. CLEAN HIT

A hard punch to the solar plexus, located in the center of the chest, can induce feelings of intense breathlessness. A blow here might even do serious internal damage to the stomach, liver, or gallbladder.

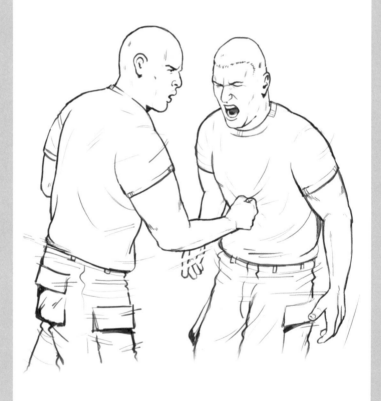

116. KIDNEY STRIKE

Around the back of the torso, two vulnerable areas are the soft sections over the kidneys. With no muscular protection, they are exposed to strong hooking punches or to knee attacks.

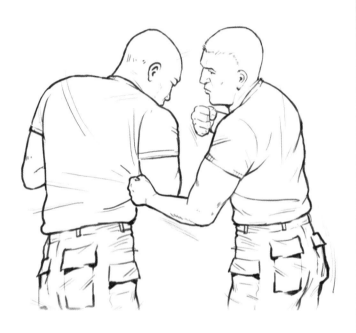

117. SPINAL COLUMN

Attacking the spinal column can have potentially lethal results. You can damage or sever the spinal cord. For these reasons, it shouldn't be targeted unless in an extreme situation.

118. TORSO STRIKES

Remember that the torso is not really vulnerable.
Blows to the torso are mainly effective for setting up
a more significant attack. They are resorted to if no
other target is obvious.

119. ELBOW JOINTS

When grappling, an opponent's elbow joints can be
locked with pain-compliance techniques. However,
the employment of the technique needs to be strong
enough to counter the opponent's bicep strength.

120. TARGETING THE ELBOW

Blows to the elbows can damage them and generate
pain compliance, but this generally works only when
blunt-force weapons are applied. Otherwise, elbow
strikes are unlikely to stop an opponent.

121. VULNERABLE THROAT

The throat is one of the most vulnerable areas of the
human body. A blow to the windpipe can result in
the collapse of the throat and the suffocation of the
victim.

122. FINGER LOCKS

The fingers can be attacked with locking, bending, or twisting actions, usually in the process of breaking a hold or lock. The little fingers can be more easily damaged than the larger fingers.

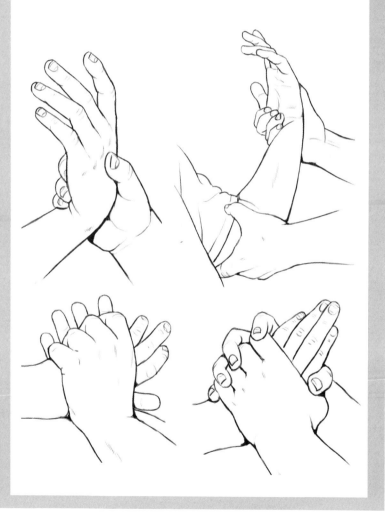

123. CAROTID ARTERIES

Compressing the carotid arteries on either side of the throat, using a choking technique, can cause unconsciousness in a matter of seconds.

124. JAWLINE HIT

One of the most influential body targets is the jawline, extending several inches on either side of the point of the jaw. This area contains groups of nerve endings that produce an instant knockout effect when struck with a well-targeted punch.

125. GLASS JAW

A blow to the side of the jaw can result in a fractured jawbone, causing intense pain and quickly stopping most fights even when there isn't a knockout.

126. BROKEN TEETH

Avoid delivering punches to your opponent's teeth. While you might be able to knock some teeth out, broken teeth can inflict deep lacerations on your hands, which are easily infected by oral bacteria.

127. KNOCKOUT BLOW

Any punch to the head area can cause a knockout by shaking the brain in the skull. The impact on the brain can lead to instant unconsciousness.

128. NOSE STRIKE

A fast blow to the nose can produce a broken nose, extensive bleeding, and watering eyes. Although nose attacks are rarely fight stoppers, they can be useful for setting up other attacks.

129. CUPPED HAND STRIKE

A blow to the ear with a cupped hand forces air into the ear canal. If delivered with enough force, this can produce a ruptured eardrum.

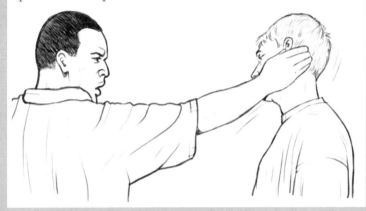

130. EAR GRAB

Ears can be tightly gripped and ripped, but in a fast-moving fight against a sweaty opponent, it can be hard to get a hold on this part of an opponent's body.

131. SOFT TARGET?

The eyes are probably the most vulnerable part of the human body, even though they are reasonably protected by the blink response. A finger jab or gouging attack on the eyes can result in temporary or permanent blindness.

132. TEMPLES

The temples can be struck with a hard hook or with cross punches to deliver a stunning effect on an opponent.

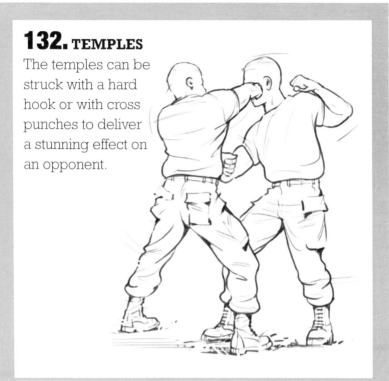

133. DOWNWARD HIT

The skull is incredibly strong and resistant to most hand-based attacks, but it is vulnerable to downward attacks by clubs and other impact weapons.

134. KEEP HITTING

Adrenaline often produces an anesthetic effect during a fight, numbing the response to pain. For this reason, don't assume that any one blow will be decisive.

135. EFFECTIVE PUNCHING

An effective punch is the product of three elements—speed (of the punch), focus (on the target), and power (the transference of body weight into the punch).

136. ON THE FRONT FOOT

Step into each punch with the front foot to add extra force to it. Make the step snappy and forceful, and coordinate the moment the step lands with the contact the fist makes to the target.

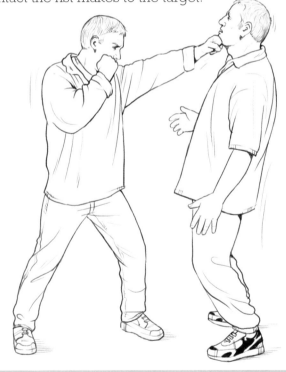

137. PUT YOUR BODY INTO IT

Think of punching with the whole body, not just an arm or a fist. At the moment of impact, tense all the muscles of the body and twist the hip and the shoulder into the target.

138. MAKING A GOOD FIST

A good punch starts by making a good fist. Tightly curl your fingers into the palm of your hand, placing your thumb on the outside of your index finger, and taking the thumb back so that it does not protrude beyond the fingers.

139. RIGID WEAPON

Squeeze the fist inward between the thumb and the little finger, making your fist a single rigid structure.

140. MIDDLE KNUCKLES

The principal point of impact on the fist should be the two large knuckles of the index finger and middle finger. When punching, the other knuckles are more liable to be broken.

141. PROPER ALIGNMENT

To protect your fist when punching, align the largest knuckle of the hand and the bones in the back of the hand, horizontally and vertically, with the bones in the forearm.

142. RELAXED MUSCLES

To achieve speed when punching, keep the muscles of the arm relaxed as the punch lands on the target. Remember that a relaxed muscle is a fast muscle.

143. PUNCH INTO THE TARGET

When the punch connects with the target, this is when and where you deliver the power, tensing your body and driving body weight into the blow.

144. PUNCH ON THROUGH

Penetration is an important component of an effective punch. Punch deeply into the target. Your focus point should be several inches beyond the surface of the skin.

145. THROWING A PUNCH

Another technique for improving the speed of a punch is to imagine that your fist is a stone that you are throwing toward the target.

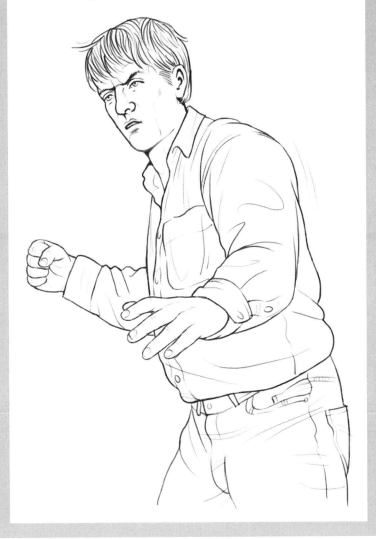

146. TWIST THE FIST

In karate and many other martial arts, the punch
is given additional penetration by twisting the fist
from a palm-up to a palm-down position during the
moment of impact, screwing the blow into the target.

147. TWIST FOR FORCE

As boxers demonstrate, a very pronounced rotational
action is not necessary for powerful penetration, but
some degree of twist aids the force of the punch.

148. ADDING WEIGHT

To add more body weight to the blow, you can push
forward off the ground with your back foot, while
fractionally lifting the front foot off the ground.

149. BODY POSITION

Your body position is critical to effective punching.
You need to put yourself in a position in which
you can easily move, retain your balance, and put
together a variety of punches.

150. BOXER'S STANCE

The classic boxer's stance is known as the orthodox stance—with feet set shoulder-width apart and with the lead foot and upper body at a 45-degree angle to the front.

151. FISTS UP, ELBOWS IN

In the orthodox stance, hold your fists up at either side of your chin, keep your elbows in to protect the body, and hold your chin low. If you are right-handed, your left foot and left fist should be forward.

152. STABLE PLATFORM

The orthodox stance enables you to move in a quick and stable manner, to punch fluidly, and to snap back from the punches into a responsive guard.

153. HIKATAE

In many martial arts, a punch delivered with one arm is given extra torsional power when the opposite hand is being pulled back to the waist with equal speed and power. This is called *hikatae*.

154. FROM THE STOMACH

Hikatae forces the puncher to deliver the power from the *hara*, or center of the stomach. Even if you don't use *hikatae*, keep the stomach muscles tensed and locked to channel power from the twisting action of the waist.

155. KEEPING YOUR GUARD

Boxers don't use *hikatae*, preferring instead to keep their guard up at all times as a form of protection. Given the utter practicality of boxing techniques, this is a sensible policy to follow.

156. TYPES OF PUNCHES

There are several different types of punches. The critical punches to master are the jab, hook, cross, and uppercut. Train intensively in them until they become second nature.

157. THE JAB

The jab is the fastest of the punches. It is delivered with the leading arm, and it is used to soften up an opponent, spoil his attacks, and set him up for more powerful techniques.

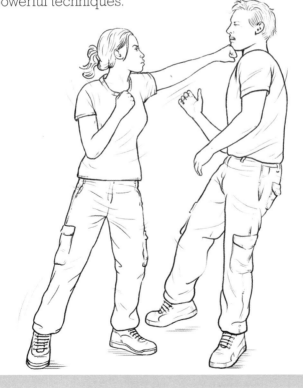

158. DELIVERING A JAB

To deliver the jab, thrust the leading fist out at a straight line toward your target, aiming for the chin or nose. Make it extremely fast and stinging, and immediately snap the fist back after delivering your power to the target.

159. PUSH IT

To make the jab more powerful and extend its range, push forward the shoulder and the hip on the same side at the moment of impact.

160. RAPID JABS

Throw rapid jabs at your opponent to disrupt his movement and ability to attack. Use the jabs to control the pace of the fight in your favor.

161. CLOSE-RANGE POWER

At particularly close ranges, the jabbing arm is often unable to fully extend into the punch. In these situations, use a small hip and torso twist combined with a drive forward with the feet to deliver body weight to the punch.

162. THE CROSS

The cross is an exceptionally powerful punch and is often used as a knockout blow once the opponent has been set up by jabbing attacks.

163. NON-LEADING FIST

The non-leading fist delivers the cross punch. For example, if you are right-handed, and your left foot and left fist are forward, then the cross comes from your right side.

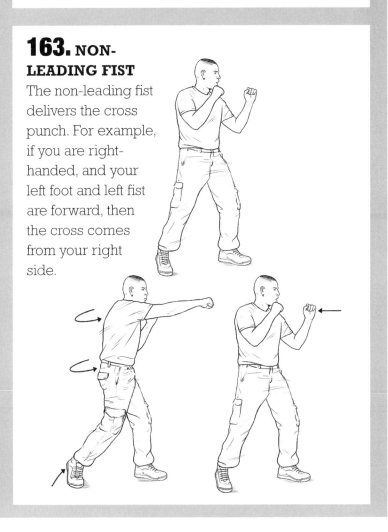

164. DELIVERING A CROSS

To deliver the cross, fire your fist out toward your target at the face (ideally at the chin), solar plexus, or lower ribs.

165. DRIVE INTO THE TARGET

At the moment the cross punch touches the target, drive your right hip forward (for a right-sided punch), straighten your right back leg, push off from the floor, and twist your right shoulder into the blow.

166. DEVASTATING HIT

If all the elements of the cross are synched together at exactly the right moment, your whole body weight will be transferred into the punch, with a potentially devastating effect.

167. HOOK PUNCH

The hook punch follows a curved path to the target, swung in from the peripheries of the opponent's vision and targeted at the ribs, kidney area, or side of the chin/head.

168. POWER FROM THE HIP

In the orthodox stance, hooks can be delivered with the left hand or the right hand. The key to both is the rapid twist of the hip into the punch to deliver the power.

169. LEFT HOOK

To deliver a left hook from a left-forward stance, throw the punch in a semicircular arc from the outside, with your elbow up and behind the punch.

170. TWIST THE HIP

As you swing your left hook into the target, push your left hip in the direction of the punch, pivoting on your feet and drawing your right hip back. This twisting action puts your body weight into the punch.

171. RIGHT HOOK

To deliver a right hook, swing the right fist in an arc toward the target, this time pushing the right hip forward and around into the blow, sharply twisting on your feet to the left.

172. THE UPPERCUT

The uppercut is a difficult punch to master, but it is very powerful, and if properly delivered it can strike your opponent with almost complete surprise.

173. CHIN HIT

Like the hook punch, the uppercut can be delivered with both the left and right hands. The impact point is the same—the underside of the chin.

174. LEFT UPPERCUT

To deliver the left uppercut, slightly bend your knees
to drop yourself below the level of your opponent's
chin. Then use the knees to push upward while
swinging the punching fist up toward the target.

175. PALM INWARD

With an uppercut, keep the palm of the punching
fist facing toward you as it travels upward. At the
moment of impact, push your left hip upward and
forward to transfer your body weight to the punch.

176. RIGHT UPPERCUT

For a right uppercut from an orthodox stance, again throw your fist (this time your right) vertically from a bended knee position. On impact, thrust the right hip forward and upward.

177. HUNCH YOUR SHOULDERS

Keep the shoulders hunched during punching techniques, with the shoulders acting as a guard for the side of the chin and face.

178. FOCUS ON THE TARGET

To improve the accuracy of your punches, sharply focus your eyes on the target area, and go for it with complete commitment.

179. ELBOWS IN

For straight punches, keep your elbows close to your body to enhance the power and to avoid "telegraphing" your punch to your opponent. If the elbow is out, your opponent is more likely to see the punch coming in.

180. STRAIGHT JABS

Practice making punches straight from your guard position. Don't pull your fist back first. This will send a clear signal to your opponent that you are about to make the punch.

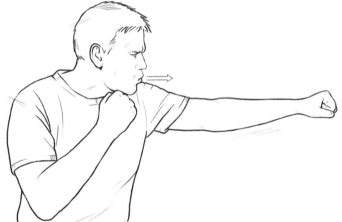

181. "BUNCHES OF PUNCHES"

In a real fight, think in terms of "bunches of punches." Deliver combinations of punches of different types to keep your opponent disoriented and to maximize the chances for a decisive blow.

182. OPEN-HAND HIT

As an alternative to clenched-fist punching, you can deliver jabs, hooks, uppercuts, and crosses with an open hand, pulling the hand back and striking with the heel of the palm.

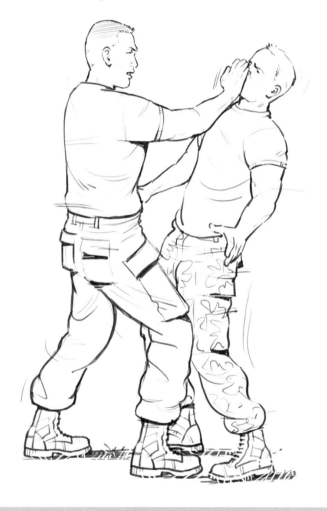

183. PALM-HEEL STRIKE

Although the palm-heel strike does not deliver the striking pain of the fist, it offers a very strong impact surface, and it limits the risk of breaking your hand.

184. TARGETS

The best targets for palm-heel strikes are the side of the chin and the temples. As you would when delivering a punch, twist your body weight into the blows.

185. FACE SLAP

A simple open-handed slap across the face, while not a knockout blow, can shock an opponent to his senses and take away his initial confidence.

186. HANDS-DOWN START

Also practice making punches from a hands-down position. You might be able to stop a fight before it's even begun with a quick cross or hook.

187. KNIFE STRIKE

Your hand is also a body weapon when used as a chopping tool for a "knife strike." Extend the fingers into a rigid "blade," and use the thick padded area of the hand on the little-finger edge as the striking surface.

188. BACKHAND KNIFE STRIKE

The backhand knife strike involves swinging the hand across the body, and then striking with the knife hand against the opponent's throat or chin. The palm should be facing downward. At the point of impact, twist the shoulders and torso into the blow.

189. FOREHAND KNIFE STRIKE

For the forehand knife strike, swing the hand from outside the body, this time with the palm facing upward. The targets are the same as the backhand strike.

190. HAMMER FIST

Another hand weapon is the hammer fist. This uses the same impact area as the knife strike, but the blow is delivered with a tightly bunched fist.

191. HAMMER STRIKE

The hammer strike is a very solid attack, and it leaves you less prone to hand damage than the knife strike. The hammer strike is used to attack the bridge of the nose and the side and back of the neck.

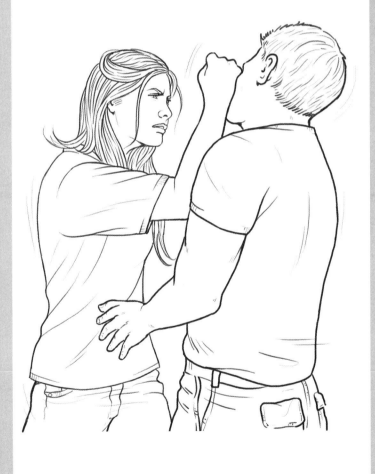

192. ELBOW STRIKES

Another important set of arm techniques are elbow strikes. As the name suggests, they are delivered with the point of the elbow. These are excellent fighting tools for close-range encounters.

193. UPPERCUT ELBOW

With the uppercut elbow strike, add body weight to the impact by pushing up from the knees and thrusting the hip on the impact side upward and into the strike.

194. ROUNDHOUSE ELBOW

The basic elbow strike is the roundhouse type. Swing the point of the elbow fast and hard at your target area, usually the side of the face or chin—or the neck.

195. TWIST INTO THE BLOW

As you do with the hook punch, give power to the elbow roundhouse strike by twisting your shoulder, torso, and hip into the blow, driving through your opponent.

196. UPPERCUT ELBOW

You can also deliver an uppercut elbow strike. Swing your fist vertically past your opponent's face, following up with an elbow strike on the underside of the chin.

197. REAR ELBOW TO RIBS

If someone grabs you from behind, you can attack by using a rear elbow strike. Push your arm out forward, and then drive it back with speed, attacking with the point of the elbow to the ribs.

198. REAR ELBOW TO FACE

The rear elbow strike can also be used to attack the opponent's face. Swing the point of the elbow backward in an arcing motion, twisting the striking-side hip to the rear to add body weight.

199. BACKFIST TECHNIQUE

Another hand-strike technique is known in martial arts as the backfist. To deliver the backfist, first aim your elbow at the target—the temple or side of the chin—and cock your clenched fist, palm down, against your bicep.

200. BACKFIST STRIKE

To launch the backfist, whip your fist out from the cocked position, rolling the fist over at the end of the extension to strike with the two main knuckles against the target area, usually the temple.

201. JAB-JAB-CROSS

A good combination of punches is the jab-jab-cross. The second jab should hit the opponent just as his head is rocking forward in recovery from the first jab. Practice the following punch combinations: jab-cross-front uppercut; front hook-cross; jab-jab-jab-hook-front uppercut; front hook-cross-jab-jab-cross.

202. FINGER JAB

Don't forget more basic hand-attack tools. Jab your fingers into the opponent's eyes. Also use your nails, if they are sharp, to make clawing attacks against the eyes or other vulnerable parts.

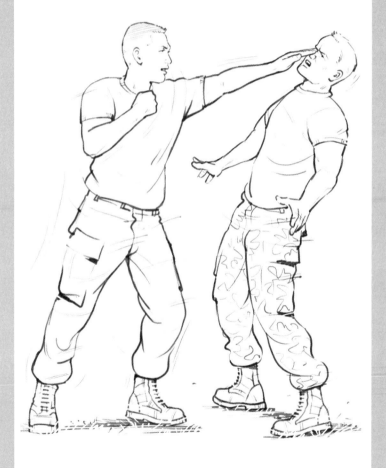

203. REAL KICKING

Real combat kicking is very different from the spectacular kicking in martial arts movies. Make sure that you deliver only kicks that are within your physical capability and that don't leave you vulnerable.

204. MAINTAIN BALANCE

Balance is critical to delivering effective kicks. Never deliver a kick that leaves you unbalanced and vulnerable to being knocked over by your opponent.

205. RESIST IMPACT

When thinking about kicking balance, keep in mind the impact of the kick on your opponent. Practice kicking techniques on a heavy bag so you can get used to the bounce-back of impact.

206. LEG SNAP-BACK

When you have delivered any type of kick, snap the leg back and quickly get it down onto the floor. Keep the time you spend on one leg to the absolute minimum.

207. LOW TARGETS

Unless you are super-fast and super-flexible, keep all your kicks targeted below the waist. By attacking areas such as the groin, thighs, knees, and shins, you can set up your opponent for follow-up punches.

208. AVOIDING THE LEG GRAB

Another virtue of kicking only below the waist is that it limits the possibility of your opponent's grabbing your leg and controlling you.

209. LEG-GRAB COUNTERATTACK

If your leg is grabbed and held, leap forward and into your opponent, sharply contracting the gripped leg, and attack the face with powerful punches or elbow strikes.

210. FRONT SNAP KICK 1

The most basic of all kicks is the front snap kick. From the classic stance, with the left foot forward, this is usually delivered with the right leg.

211. FRONT SNAP KICK 2

To begin the front snap kick, move the knee of your kicking leg up toward the target, drawing your kicking foot off the floor in a whiplike action.

212. FRONT SNAP KICK 3

Continue the front snap kick once your knee is lifted toward the target. Snap your lower leg out and drive the top of your foot into the target area, typically the stomach or groin.

213. FRONT SNAP KICK 4

The moment you contact your opponent with the front snap kick, push your hips forward and into the target, transferring your body weight. Do not lean too far forward, in case you lose balance.

214. FOLLOW THROUGH

The front snap kick is one of the fastest kicks, and one of the easiest to master. It is relatively easy to control balance while delivering this kick. After the foot makes contact, it is simple enough to step forward from the kick and to begin a punching or grappling technique.

215. ACCELERATION

Although the snap kick is being described in separate stages, think of it as one fluid, powerful move, with the kicking foot accelerating into the target from the moment it leaves the floor.

216. LOW BLOW

You can use a short, flicking version of the front snap kick to make a lightning-quick kick to your opponent's shin, the pain of which can force him to drop his guard.

217. ROUNDHOUSE KICK

For attacking body targets from the side, the best technique is the classic roundhouse kick. This kick is ideal for attacking an opponent's groin, stomach, solar plexus, or—and only if you are very flexible—the head.

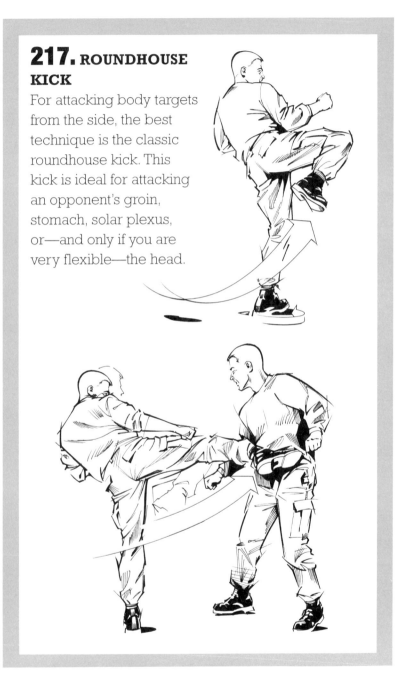

218. ROUNDHOUSE 1

To make the roundhouse kick from a classic stance, with the left leg forward, raise the right knee up the side of the body with the leg cocked back. At the same time, begin spinning the body around to the left, pivoting on the left foot.

219. ROUNDHOUSE 2

Maintain the momentum of the spin. As the kicking knee moves around to point at the target, whip the lower leg out and drive the top of the foot into the target.

220. ROUNDHOUSE 3

At the point of impact, roll your upper hip into the kick to add a little more weight behind it. Keep your shoulders at 45 degrees toward the target. Your supporting foot should point 45 degrees to the rear.

221. ROUNDHOUSE 4

Make sure you kick through the target for maximum impact. For example, if you are kicking the left side of your opponent's body, aim to drive the kick all the way through to his right side.

222. ROUNDHOUSE 5

To add extra power to the pivot of the roundhouse, step with your left foot farther to the left side just before doing the pivot, adding the sideways motion of the body to the kick.

223. ROUNDHOUSE 6

Once you have delivered the roundhouse kick, use the twisting tension stored between the shoulders and the hips to drive your kicking leg back to the right and down to the floor.

224. ROUNDHOUSE 7

Throughout the roundhouse kick, keep the knee of your supporting leg bent a little for stability. Also keep the movement on a level plane throughout. Don't bob up and down during the kick.

225. FAST ROUNDHOUSE

Like the front snap kick, you can also deliver a fast roundhouse from the front leg. However, this technique is more commonly seen in martial arts competitions than in street fights.

226. SWIFT STAMP

If an attacker is standing very close to you, short stamping kicks to his knees, legs, ankles, or feet can be very useful. These will be instantly painful and may cause your opponent to hesitate.

227. SIDE THRUST 1

The side thrust kick is a technique that delivers a strong pushing action against an opponent. It can be used to drive an opponent away, or as a painful attack against thighs, knees, and shins.

228. SIDE THRUST 2

From the classic stance, the side thrust kick begins
by lifting the knee sharply upward and directly
forward, aiming at your opponent.

229. SIDE THRUST 3

To continue the side thrust kick, as the knee reaches
the front of its lift, in the high position, pivot on
the supporting foot and thrust out the kicking leg
directly into the target.

230. SIDE THRUST 4

Like the roundhouse kick, deliver the side thrust kick
without bobbing up and down. Keep low, and drive
the momentum forward into the kick.

231. SIDE THRUST 5

To give the kick power, you should strongly push the kicking hip into the target, rolling it so that the hip and leg are locked into a full extension.

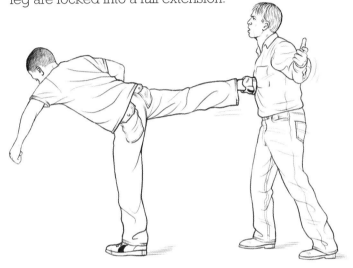

232. SIDE THRUST 6

The impact point of the side thrust kick is the heel of the foot, or the upper side of the foot, known as the blade.

233. WAIST-LEVEL TARGET

Because of the extension of the thrust kick, it leaves you vulnerable to being grabbed by the opponent. For this reason, it is better to keep the kick below waist level.

234. SPINNING KICK

A more complex kick is the reverse roundhouse. In a real fight situation, this should only be used if you are an expert martial artist.

235. REVERSE ROUNDHOUSE 1

From a classic stance (left foot forward), the reverse roundhouse kick begins when you pivot sharply on your feet, twisting to the left. Quickly snap your head around to look at the target over your right shoulder.

236. REVERSE ROUNDHOUSE 2

As you twist around, lift the knee of the kicking leg (your right) up and out to the side. Maintain the spinning momentum, and swing the knee and foot up toward the impact point.

237. REVERSE ROUNDHOUSE 3

Straighten the kicking leg out and strike the target with the heel or the sole of the foot. Maintain the spin for the follow-through.

238. REVERSE THRUST KICK 1

An alternative to the reverse roundhouse kick is the reverse thrust kick. From a classic stance, execute a twist on the spot, like the reverse roundhouse, but this time lift your leg straight up and to the rear.

239. REVERSE THRUST KICK 2

From the twist position, thrust your kicking leg straight through and behind, hitting the target with the ball of the foot and thrusting backward with the hip to apply leverage.

240. CHOOSE YOUR KICK

There are many types of kicks in the martial arts, but some of them have limited power and are suitable only for use in competition. Your most useful kicks are the front snap kick and reverse roundhouse. Kicking out from the floor is also often the only way of keeping an attacker at bay.

241. UPPER-BODY BALANCE

If you find that you're overbalancing during a kick, the problem might actually be your upper-body control rather than your lower-limb balance.

242. LONG-RANGE TECHNIQUE

Remember that a kick, fully extended, is a long-range technique. Ensure that you have the space to deliver it convincingly. Look out for any objects that might interfere with the kick.

243. TIMING

Timing is very important for effective kicking. The best moment to attack is when your opponent momentarily pauses between movements, which leaves him unable to react quickly to the kick.

244. UPRIGHT BODY

It is critical that you maintain balance throughout a kick. Keep the upper body as upright as possible with the arms in a stable guard position; your arms will help you maintain your balance. Always avoid the temptation to boost the height of the kick by leaning backward.

245. HEDGE YOUR BETS

Don't expect a kick, however powerful, to immediately end a fight. Always incorporate the kick within a variety of other techniques, such as punches and strikes, or use the kick to drive in closer for a grappling attack.

246. DEAD LEG STRIKES

If a fight is prolonged, you can use repeated kicks against your opponent's calves and thighs to deaden the legs and reduce mobility. Attack these areas using your shinbone rather than your feet, and keep aiming for the same point of impact to maximize the deadening effect.

247. KNEES AND SWEEPS

You don't have to use your legs just for kicking. Other applications of leg attacks are knee strikes and sweeps, the latter being particularly useful against inexperienced opponents.

248. KNEE-STRIKE TARGETS

The knees are potent close-range weapons for striking at the groin, thighs, stomach, or kidney areas. For the groin and stomach, simply lift your knee fast and drive it upward into the target area.

249. UPWARD BODY WEIGHT

As with any technique, when delivering an upward knee strike you need to sink your body weight into it to have maximum effect. To do this, push forward and upward with the hips to deliver additional lower-body weight to the blow. Feel like you are driving the blow through your opponent's rear.

250. ROUNDHOUSE KNEES

In close grappling situations, you can use both of your knees to make roundhouse-style blows to your opponent's kidney areas. Swing the knee out and high to the side, and then quickly drive the knee into the side of your opponent. Grab and control your opponent's head and neck while delivering the strikes, pulling the head into the direction of impact.

251. KNEE THRUST

Another variation of the knee strike is the knee thrust, which delivers the knee in a straight-line blow rather than an upward swinging action. Lift the knee high, and then thrust it straight out into the lower ribs or groin, pushing forward with the hips to add power. Make the knee lift and the thrusting action almost simultaneous with each other.

252. SWEEPING

Learn the art of sweeping, which refers to the act of pulling your opponent's legs out from under him, causing him either to stumble or to fall to the ground.

253. SWEEPING OPPORTUNITY

A good sweep can put your opponent on his back, giving you the opportunity to escape or to follow up with a finishing technique.

254. OPENING THE GUARD

If you destabilize your opponent with a sweep, this is a good moment to deliver a punching attack, as his arms will drop to brace himself against falling.

255. SWEEP 1

To begin a basic sweep from a classic stance, push out with your left foot and hook your instep around the back of your opponent's ankle, just below the calf.

256. SWEEP 2

To execute the sweep, pull and slightly lift your foot, lifting your opponent's leg off the floor and either sweeping it across his body or pulling it forward. Take the leg the optimal distance to throw his balance.

257. FINISHING MOVE

Once someone is on the floor, you can—only if necessary—take him out of the fight with a kick or stamp to one of the key vulnerable points.

258. STAMPING ATTACKS

Stamping attacks can be useful when directed against the feet or shins. When stamping on toes, drop your full body weight into the blow, slightly screwing your foot to maximize pain and damage.

259. SHIN SCRAPE

You can also convert a stamping attack into a scraping attack against the shin. Grind the edge of your boot or shoe straight down the shinbone, leaning toward your opponent's body to maximize contact.

260. DODGING ATTACKS

The best defense against an opponent's kicks and punches is to avoid them. It is always better to dodge attacks rather than block them.

261. FAST FOOTWORK

Throughout a confrontation, make yourself a difficult target. Keep altering the distance between your opponent and yourself by using fast footwork.

262. CLASSIC STANCE

Positioning your feet in the classic stance is crucial. They should be shoulder-width apart, with one leg extended forward. Keep your feet pointing in roughly the one o'clock position in relation to your opponent.

263. FORWARD SHUFFLE

To move forward in the classic stance, quickly shuffle your front foot forward, and immediately bring your rear foot forward as well to adjust the distance between them.

264. BACKWARD SHUFFLE

To move backward in the classic stance, rapidly move your rear foot backward, and then move your front foot back to adjust the distance between your feet.

265. SIDEWAYS SHUFFLE

You can also quickly move from side to side in a classic stance, pushing off with your front or rear foot to move in the required direction.

266. FOOTWORK PRACTICE

Constantly practice footwork, training yourself to move out of the way of incoming attacks and to quickly move into position to deliver long-, medium-, and short-range counterattacks.

267. MOVE OUTSIDE

When your opponent launches a kick, avoid it by making a quick 45-degree movement to the outside of the kick. So, if the attacker kicks with his right leg, dodge it by moving to the right side of his body.

268. COUNTERATTACK

When you move to the outside position, your opponent is placed in an awkward position to defend against your follow-up hook and cross punches.

269. THE "SLIP"

When dealing with straight punches, one of the best avoidance techniques is what boxers call the "slip." Pop your head out of the way by punching down and to the side with one shoulder, dropping your body a little at the same time.

270. SMALL MOVEMENTS

You can perform the slip on both sides of your body in the classic stance. Even just a little movement can make the difference between your taking a punch or watching the punch pass by you.

271. DROP AND SLIP

To give more power and force to the slip, scrunch down with your abdominal muscles in the direction you're heading. Bend the knees to provide further movement, but move only enough to avoid the punch.

272. SLIP AND COUNTERPUNCH

The slip has the added bonus of setting up your body to do a powerful counterpunch technique as you recover from the move. Step forward as you slip. This will put you in a good range for punching.

273. SLIP AND SLIDE

You can also slide to the side during a slip, exposing your opponent to a hook to the body or the side of the head.

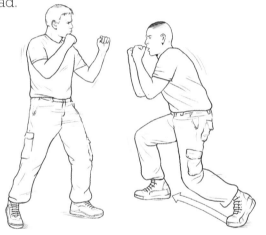

274. ROCK YOUR HEAD

In addition to the slip, you can also avoid long-range punches simply by rocking your head backward, although this should be supplemented by footwork that takes you out of the danger zone.

275. DUCKING AND DIVING

A combination of constantly moving footwork, slips, shoulder rolls, head rolls, and counterattacking will make you a complicated target for your opponent.

276. VARY THE RANGE

Be aware of distancing at all times during a fight. If your opponent has a longer reach than you do, move just outside his range, and then slip through his attacks to deliver a counterattack combination. Then escape back out of range.

277. DEFENSIVE GUARD

The best defense for your head and body is a solid
guard position. Hold your fists up at either side of
your chin, but not too closely. Hold them a short
distance out from your chest. Keep your elbows in to
protect the sides of your body.

278. CHIN DOWN

In the guard position, you should also keep your
chin down at all times and your shoulders slightly
hunched to protect the sides of your jawline.

279. HEAD GUARD

Your arms and shoulders will serve to deflect and
smother blows as they come in. However, don't let
your opponent pound your arms until they are numb.

280. WATCH AND MOVE

When you are slipping punches from the guard
position, always remember to keep your eyes on
your opponent. Don't be tempted to "hide" in
your guard.

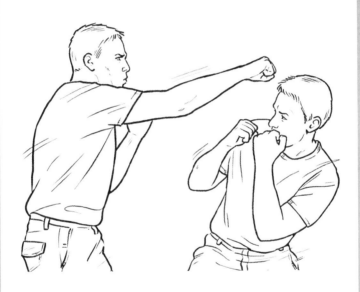

281. BLOCKING TECHNIQUES

There is a range of classic blocking techniques from
the martial arts. Remember that the purpose of a
block is to deflect and guide the attack away with
minimal contact and effort.

282. BLOCKING A JAB

To block an incoming jab punch, quickly use either an open hand or the elbow of your guard to parry the punch just to the side of your head. Make the action snap.

283. BLOCKING A HOOK

To block a hook punch, step in the opposite direction of the incoming punch, and raise both forearms to block the punch as it swings in.

284. BLOCK TO GRAPPLE

From the double-arm block, you can quickly move into a grappling technique against your opponent's arm or head.

285. BLOCKING A STRAIGHT PUNCH 1

You can block a straight punch by pivoting your forearm from inside to outside across your body, setting up your opponent to receive a hook or a cross response.

286. BLOCKING A STRAIGHT PUNCH 2

Alternatively, you can use your forearm to push your opponent's fist across his body, leaving him exposed to a cross from the outside position.

287. BE WARY

Blocking a kick is dangerous because of the power of the legs. Watch that you don't point your fingers down into the kick, as you will likely get broken fingers if you do.

288. BLOCKING A KICK

When the kick is coming in, avoid it with footwork, and if it's close, hook it to the side with your forearm, using a strike that goes downward and to the side. This technique can render your opponent off balance.

289. TWIST YOUR WRIST

To add power to a block, strongly twist your wrist into the attacking limb at the point of impact. This gives a snapping effect and adds extra power to your muscles.

290. FOOT BLOCK

In some instances, you can use your foot to smother a kick before it starts. If you are close enough when the opponent's leg lifts, you can lift up your lead foot and stifle the kick at the ankle. Do this only if the kick is just beginning.

291. OPEN GUARD

If you are threatened by someone but you don't know whether he will attack or not, raise your hands into a loose guard position, with the hands open. This is called the "open guard."

292. OPEN GUARD STANCE

The open guard looks nonthreatening, but it actually allows you to control the distance between your opponent and yourself. In addition, it can be quickly converted into attacking moves.

293. "BACK OFF!"

During an open guard phase, you can also use your front hand to push your opponent away from you. Do this with hard and sharp movements, and punctuate the push with a harsh shout such as, "Back off!"

294. KEEP YOUR DISTANCE

If your opponent pushes against the front hand of your open guard, firmly place your hand on his chest and step backward to create more distance.

295. DEFENSE TO ATTACK

If your opponent pushes into your open guard twice, forcing you to move back again, then immediately go on the attack. Convert your open hands into fists and launch into punching attacks.

296. PIVOTING MOVEMENT

Practice making strong pivoting movements with your feet. Quickly turn to one side by pivoting on one foot, pushing hard with the hip and shoulders to accelerate the turn.

297. PIVOT AND STRIKE

Pivoting motions are good for moving out of the direction of a kick, and they can also put you in an advantageous position to deliver a counterstrike.

298. WATCH THE SPACE

When you are moving during a fight, have a peripheral awareness of your surroundings at all times. Make sure that you don't move into a place where you are physically cornered.

299. OBSTRUCTIONS

Also be aware of tables, chairs, curbs, or any other objects that might cause you to stumble and fall during the fight.

300. PROTECT YOUR HEAD

During combat, make sure that you focus your defensive moves on protecting your most vulnerable areas, especially the head. Punches to the upper arm might be painful, but they are generally not serious.

301. WATERWHEEL DEFENSE

One unorthodox blocking technique is to rapidly circle your arms, waterwheel fashion, in front of your body, smacking down on everything that comes in. This could be the first line of response to a sudden, unexpected attack.

302. "RAMPAGE BLOCK"

Another way to block rapid-fire punches is to—when a left-hand punch is coming in—snap your right elbow up and place your right fist around the rear of your head, with the point of the elbow in front of your chin. This has been called the "rampage block."

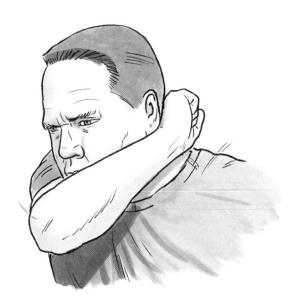

303. RAMPAGE BLOCK 2

By using the blocking technique against rapid-fire punches, you create an angular deflection surface with your forearm, and your chin is still protected.

304. RAMPAGE BLOCK 3

When applying the aforementioned technique, don't block your vision. You should be able to watch your opponent across your forearm.

305. RAMPAGE BLOCK 4

The rampage block can be used with alternating hands, blocking as fast as the opponent punches.

306. RAMPAGE BLOCK 5

When using the rampage block, place your fist around the back of your head, but leave a gap between your wrist and your skull, so there is space to soak up the impacts.

307. DAMAGE LIMITATION

Don't rely on blocks for too long. Even when deflecting or absorbing blows, you are still taking damage.

308. BLOCK AT THE WRISTS

When blocking or parrying a punch, aim to make contact with the opponent's wrist, as you will have the greatest leverage on the arm at that point.

309. FIRM GRIP

When grappling with an opponent, it is critical that you maintain a firm grip. Don't take hold of thin pieces of clothing that will tear when strained.

310. CENTER OF GRAVITY

Try to maintain a low center of gravity while grappling, as this will help you to get leverage from your leg muscles, and you will also be better able to maintain your balance.

311. PROTECT THE HANDS

If you couple your hands together in a grip, don't interlock the fingers together. If your opponent pulls the fingers apart, you are likely to damage your knuckles. Instead, lock your fingers together in a monkey grip, or grip your arms at the wrists.

312. BENT ELBOWS

Keep your elbows softly bent during any grappling maneuver. A bent elbow allows you to quickly and easily apply leverage to the grip.

313. GRIP HOLDS

When facing and gripping an opponent with both hands, you can either mirror the grip on both sides—that is, make both hands grip the collar—or place your hands on a diagonal so they are opposite each other. For example, you can place one hand on the collar and the other hand on the sleeve, to get angular leverage.

314. CHOKEHOLD

A simple chokehold is the "half nelson" of wrestling fame. Quickly move behind your opponent, and then wrap your right arm around your opponent's throat, anchoring it by locking your right hand into the crook of your left elbow.

315. CREATE AN OPENING

Use other techniques to create an opening to apply a grapple or a choke. If both your hands are gripping your opponent, for example, you can use a head butt to the nose to stun your attacker.

316. REAR CHOKE

When applying a rear choke, place your left hand around the back of your opponent's head, solidly locking the grip so the bony part of your right forearm is pressing against the front of his throat.

317. END THE FIGHT

Always remember that the intention of a grappling attack is pain compliance or, as in the case of a chokehold, unconsciousness or submission. Apply the technique until the fight is settled—that is, when your opponent is no longer capable of resistance.

318. OPPONENT PANIC

During a choke attack, your opponent will start panicking and clawing at your fingers and eyes, often with immense strength, as he begins to panic. To frustrate his attacks, keep moving on your feet and kneeing his legs, throwing him off balance and preventing his recovery.

319. SCISSOR CHOKEHOLD

To perform the front "scissor" chokehold, cross your arms at the wrists, and grab opposite sides of your opponent's shirt or coat collar, as far around the back of his neck as you can go. Now pull your elbows outward, which drives your forearms into the sides of his throat.

320. HEADLOCK

During a grappling action, try to control the movement of your opponent's head and neck. You can lock your hands around the back of the neck, squeezing the elbows and drawing your opponent's head downward.

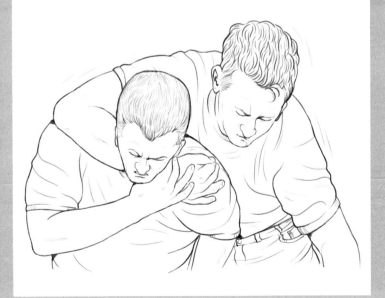

321. BODY WEIGHT

Always use body weight to your advantage when
grappling, both to exhaust and to unbalance your
opponent, and to give you the advantage when you
make your attack. Keep your weight pressed onto
your opponent, making it harder for him to control
you. Make sure, however, that you aren't vulnerable
to being thrown—stay upright.

322. GUILLOTINE CHOKEHOLD

From a neck control position, sharply snap your
opponent's head down, and whip your right forearm
underneath the throat while pinning the top of the
skull under your right armpit. You are now in a
position to apply a "guillotine" chokehold. This is
a dangerous technique to use, and should only be
applied in extreme situations.

323. HEAD CONTROL

To deliver a guillotine chokehold, lever your right
forearm upward against your opponent's throat.
Lock your right hand on your left forearm, and use
the left arm to apply more intense lift. Keep the head
controlled against your body.

324. SIDE CHOKE

You can apply a chokehold from your opponent's side, locking his head against the side of your torso. His natural instinct in this position will be to attack your groin. Keep turning your body to prevent him from getting into an attacking position.

325. CHOKE DANGER

Release the chokehold if you sense your opponent ceasing to struggle and slipping into unconsciousness. Holding a chokehold beyond this point, even by just a few seconds, can result in death, particularly if the choke is applied against neck arteries on the side of the throat.

326. GRAPPLING MARTIAL ARTS

There are dozens of individual grappling techniques available. One of the best martial arts for learning these techniques is the Brazilian style of jujitsu.

327. GROUNDWORK

Plenty of grappling takes place during groundwork fighting. Here, your objective is to either (a) place your opponent into a chokehold, (b) lock one of his limbs to force pain compliance, or (c) control his ability to move and escape your lock.

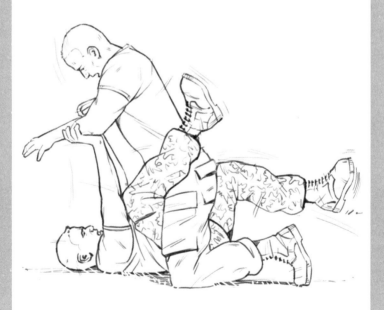

328. PROTECT THE THROAT

Make sure that you guard your own neck during a grappling fight, as you want to avoid being placed in a chokehold at all costs. Keep your eyes glued to your opponent, watching his hands at all times. Try to maintain proper guard, or at least keep your arms up and your chin down, with your shoulders hunched up.

329. RELAX YOUR MUSCLES

During a grappling contest, try to relax your body as much as possible. This will enable you to move faster, and it can also help you to tolerate higher levels of pain. Keep breathing at all times—your muscles need a good supply of oxygen to maintain their strength and efficiency.

330. LEG CONTROL

If an opponent is on top of you, wrap your legs around his torso and use your powerful leg muscles to keep him off balance and unable to apply much power to his punches. Keep twisting your legs from side to side, constantly and awkwardly shifting his body weight and making it difficult for him to control you at any point.

331. FORCE A ROLL

If you are pinned by an opponent on the floor, don't push straight against his body weight and line of grip. Instead, look for places you can push with both arms to force your opponent's body to roll in the direction you want.

332. LOCKING THE ARM

When performing a side choke from the floor position, you can use your non-choking hand to pin your opponent's punching arm across his chest. This will enforce a higher degree of compliance.

333. SHIFTING WEIGHT

When trying to escape from a grappling technique, use your legs and shift your body posture to create angles that unsettle your opponent's balance.

334. HEAD PULL

When straddling an opponent, you can force compliance by reaching down, grabbing his skull with both hands, and forcing his chin to his chest. If you apply this grip with both arms, your opponent will struggle to move.

335. ANGLES OF DEFENSE

If you are thrown onto your back, use your legs to push your body into angles that make it difficult for your opponent to control you on the ground.

336. ARMLOCK

A simple armlock, which can be applied in seconds, involves scooping your right arm under your opponent's left armpit and then twisting to your left. Lock his left arm so it is straight against your shoulders, using your right arm for leverage.

337. FINGER LOCKS

Locks can also be applied on a small scale. Individual fingers can be bent backward to control your opponent's hands and to force pain compliance.

338. LEVERAGE FROM THE FEET

Keep on the balls of your feet during a grappling contest. This position will allow you to apply maximum leverage.

339. LARYNX GRAB

Another useful chokehold is the larynx grab. Form
your hand into a strong pinching mechanism, and
then reach forward to grab your opponent's larynx,
the section of the throat that is just beneath the chin.
Pinch the larynx while pushing him backward.

340. CLEAN MOVES

When you perform a grappling attack, act calmly
and deliberately. Don't be tempted to rush the move,
as the outcome of a poorly applied grapple can be
worse than responding with panic and no technique
at all.

341. BREAK FALLS

In addition to learning how to throw an opponent, you should also learn how to perform break falls— protecting your body against impact if you are thrown to the ground.

342. BACKWARD BREAK FALL

One of the simplest break falls to perform is the backward break fall, to be used if you are thrown directly onto your back. As you fall backward, bend your knees and throw both arms out to the sides, slapping the ground just before your torso strikes.

343. SIDE BREAK FALL

The side break fall is a variation of the backward version, to be used if you are thrown onto the side of your body. In this instance, slap the ground just before impact with the arm closest to the ground. The slapping action limits the speed of your impact.

344. OPPOSITE FORCE

Many throws can be combined with the sweeping actions described earlier. For example, if you sweep your opponent's right leg from your left to your right, you can grab his left collar and right arm at the same time and throw his upper body down in the opposite direction to the sweep.

345. OUTER REAPING THROW

Another type of classic throwing attack is the outer reaping throw. Hook your right leg behind your opponent's right knee, and at the same time push him backward against his shoulders and chin. Slightly lift your hooking leg for maximum effect.

346. INNER REAPING THROW

A variation of the outer reaping throw is the inner reaping throw. In this instance, hook your right leg behind your opponent's left leg, lifting the leg off the ground while simultaneously pushing your opponent's torso backward.

347. HEAD-BUTT SETUP

You can extend the effect of any reaping attack by proceeding with a stunning head-butt, disorienting your opponent and leaving him more susceptible to the subsequent throw to the ground.

348. PREPARING TO FALL

When making any throw, be aware that your opponent will probably maintain a strong grip on your clothing as he goes down. If you are going to fall with him, ensure that you stay on top, adding your body weight to the impact your opponent feels on the ground.

349. HIP THROW 1

One of the most effective throws in self-defense is the hip throw. Quickly turn your body around, with both of your feet inside your opponent's feet and with your buttocks tightly pushed into his groin. At the same time you take this position, loop your right arm around his torso and grab his right sleeve with your left arm.

350. HIP THROW 2

To complete the hip throw, quickly whip your
opponent over your right hip, pushing up with your
knees at the same time to lift your opponent up and
over, so he falls onto his back. Make sure that your
knees are well bent during the setup stage of this
maneuver.

351. OFF-BALANCE

When you set up any throw, try to disrupt your opponent's balance before moving in to implement the technique. A quick shove or a pull on the shoulders can momentarily put him off-balance and leave him less able to resist your subsequent attack.

352. SHOULDER THROW

There is an advanced and powerful throw called the shoulder throw. It is set up in a similar way to the hip throw. However, your right arm is hooked beneath your opponent's right armpit, and you use this arm plus a knee thrust upward to lever him up and over your shoulders.

353. TRIP-THROW

A simple trip-throw involves swinging your right leg across the front of your opponent, pushing your back against the front of his torso. Rigidly anchor your right leg on the floor at a 45-degree angle and then, after gripping your opponent around his torso, throw him over the outstretched leg.

354. LEG THROW

One particularly effective throw is the leg throw. Facing your opponent, rapidly squat down and reach forward to grab behind both of his knees with your hands. Quickly stand, sweeping his legs from the floor while simultaneously using your shoulders to push his torso backward.

355. CONTROL THE ARMS

During any throw, try to control your attacker's arms throughout the move. When he hits the floor, he is liable to panic and start thrashing. You have less chance of receiving a blow if his arms are immediately locked under control.

356. GROUND DEFENSE

If you do find yourself on the ground after being thrown or following a stumble, draw your legs in and maintain a high guard with your arms to protect against subsequent kicking attacks. Try to get to your feet as quickly as possible; kick out to give yourself a brief window in which to stand up.

357. SPORTS TACKLE

One elementary throw is basically a variation of a classic football tackle. Dive at your opponent's waist, hitting this area of his body with a shoulder. Meanwhile, wrap your arms around his back. Your momentum should knock him to the floor.

358. ROLLING DEFENSE

If you are attacked with a tackle dive, you can roll backward while bending over at the waist. Apply a lock around your opponent's stomach with both arms. Maintain the roll on the floor, flipping your attacker up and over your head.

359. FOOT MOVEMENTS

Also observe the position of your opponent's feet as you move around and toward him. Throws are best delivered when his feet have crossed over, when they are close together, or when he is making a step, as he is easily thrown off balance at these times.

360. CLOTHING GRAB

Assess whether the strength and thickness of your opponent's clothing will prevent you from making an effective throw. For example, an official judo *gi* is made from strong fabric that can be easily gripped and pulled, whereas a standard fashion shirt is fragile and will tear easily, rather than provide the needed leverage.

361. BELT THROW

Certain items of clothing can help you implement
a throw. For example, if your opponent is wearing
a strong belt, you can use it to apply leverage.
Spin around behind him, put your arms in front
of his torso, and grab the front of his belt. Then lift
him upward and backward. A clothing grab is also
useful if you wish to lift and throw an opponent
from behind.

362. LEG GRAB

Timing is critical to performing an effective throw. Look for a point at which your opponent is momentarily destabilized or distracted, such as following a punching or kicking attack. For example, you might be able to grab your opponent's leg following a failed kick, then push into him and disrupt his balance.

363. GET HIM MOVING

Before delivering a throw, get your opponent moving, as it is always easier to lift and throw a moving object than a static object. Push and pull him erratically to get his torso swaying and off-balance.

364. CONFIDENT THROW

Throws can be complicated to execute and need to be performed with total confidence, bred from repeating the maneuver many times in a training setting. Don't attempt to throw your opponent unless you are sure you can put yourself in the precise position needed to make the throw effective.

365. GROUND SLAM

If the impact of slamming your opponent on the ground temporarily stuns him, take advantage of his pain and disorientation. Use this moment as an opportunity to escape or to deliver a finishing blow, such as a stomp or knee drop.

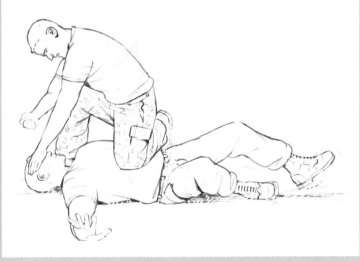

366. DESCENDING FORCE

Make sure that you keep control of your opponent while he is in the air, but then use the power of your arms and your descending body weight to slap him to the ground forcefully. Remember to use your whole body in the throw, and rely more on smoothly applied principles of leverage rather than just brute strength.

367. GRIP POINTS

Use a varied combination of grips. The classic grip points are the upper sleeve, the collar, the back of the neck, and the belt.

368. DON'T STARE AT THE FEET

A common mistake a person can make when preparing to execute a throw is to stare at the opponent's feet. This gives your opponent clues about what you are thinking. It can also distract you from other attacks.

369. USE LEVERAGE

Don't rely on pure muscle power to deliver a throw. Good throwing technique comes from principles of leverage, not simply sheer strength.

370. PICK YOUR MOMENT

When grappling, try to feel your opponent's direction of movement and balance through your grip. Learn to read the right moment to execute a throw.

371. PUNCH, THEN CLOSE

Always remember that you can use a throw in combination with a variety of other attacks and defensive moves. For example, you can launch a defense with an explosive shower of punches, then close the distance and implement your throw.

372. DANGEROUS ODDS

Do not let movie representations of fighting fool you into thinking that you can battle multiple attackers effortlessly. The odds against your success increase as the number of attackers increases.

373. GROUP LEADER

Try to assess the dynamics of any threatening group. Attempt to identify the group leader, and figure out whether any group members seem less than willing to engage in violence. If you take out the leader, the others may be less willing to get into a fight.

374. USE OBSTACLES

One advantage you have is that it is easier for an individual to move through obstacles than it is for a group. Try to find escape routes that make it awkward for the group to follow you, such as through doorways or alleys.

375. CHANNEL THE ATTACKS

If you are cornered, look for a location where the members of the group cannot attack you simultaneously, such as in a recessed doorway.

376. KEEP MOVING

Don't give the group enough time to surround you. If you keep moving, the attackers have to constantly readjust their fight plan.

377. FIGHT AVOIDANCE

If the chance presents itself, avoid a fight by talking with one or more reasonable members of the group. Don't level any accusations against the rest of the group in the process.

378. PSYCHOLOGICAL EFFECT

When defending yourself against a group attack, go berserk as a form of pyschological deterrent, screaming, salivating, and striking at any target that enters your range of vision. Don't allow the group to think that they have an easy victim, as that will just encourage their attacks more.

379. ALL-AROUND AWARENESS

Maintain awareness of what is going on around you, in case other members of the group are getting ready to attack. Also be aware of bystanders, as sometimes third parties can suddenly join a group attack for little apparent reason.

380. FOCUS THE FIGHT

Fight in focused bursts of violent energy. Position your body so you can engage one of the individuals with total commitment, delivering a short and vicious barrage of attacks to take him out of the fight. Then break away, pause, and engage someone else—try to control the pace of the clash.

381. HIT FIRST

If it looks as though the group is going to attack and you can't escape, go on the offensive first, before they can recover. Use a particularly violent maneuver to take out at least one or two of the attackers before they can coordinate their efforts.

382. SET THE RANGE

Use your arms to control the distance between your attackers and yourself. Keep your guard up and shove away anyone who gets too close. Set your opponents at your ideal punching range.

383. TAKEDOWN TECHNIQUES

Make your attacks as precise as possible, aiming only for vulnerable points. Use your punching techniques to go for clear knockouts. Seeing one of their friends knocked unconscious can dissuade the rest of the group from further prosecuting their attack.

384. SUCKER PUNCH

Many group attacks begin with a sucker punch.
Watch out for anyone who tries moving into your
range. Look for telltale signs of the sucker punch,
such as twitching hands and arms, or the moment
when an attacker makes a pretense of scratching his
own face.

385. USE THE TERRAIN

Wherever the fight takes place, use the terrain to
your advantage. If you can get higher than your
opponents—up a flight of stairs, for example—you
can use the height advantage and the narrow width
of the staircase to control the attack.

386. NECK CLINCH 1

Grab one of the group members in a neck clinch
to control his body. You can then maneuver him
as a shield between the other attackers and yourself.
Keep kneeing the clinched opponent to subdue
his punches.

387. NECK CLINCH 2

To apply an effective clinch, squeeze your elbows together to increase the lock on your opponent's head and jawline. The elbows also function as a guard against your opponent's body shots and uppercuts.

388. NECK CLINCH 3

Maintain movement to keep your opponent off-balance. Keep driving him backward into the other members of the group. Drag him around in circles.

389. NECK CLINCH 4

Apply the clinch-shield technique to the smallest and least muscular member of the attacking group. Select someone you can easily control—but don't think you can hold him forever. At some point you will need to drop him and fight the others.

390. KEEP IN SIGHT

During the buildup to a group fight, try to keep the whole group in front of you, so you can see the position of each member. As they move, readjust your position as needed—pulling back away from the group will usually force them to align with you head-on.

391. USE A WEAPON

Even with effective techniques, the odds are stacked against you with multiple attackers. If possible, try to acquire a weapon, one that shows your attackers you are prepared to fight back with total violence. Make sure that it is a weapon you can wield quickly, as speed is the life-saver.

392. FLANKING ATTACKS

Don't let yourself be flanked by your attackers. If you are flanked to the side, you might need to punch through the group to the other side, to break up the pincer effort.

393. NO PITY

During the buildup to the fight, don't think that the group will take pity on you because they outnumber you. Groups often have a stronger tendency toward violence than individuals.

394. PROTECTIVE ZONE

If you can get hold of a weapon, a long stick or club is ideal. You can use the weapon to create a protective zone around you, striking at anyone who ventures into your zone.

395. STAY OUT OF TROUBLE

Don't be drawn into altercations between groups, as you are likely to become a victim. Call the police rather than get involved.

396. FIGHT DIRTY

In a group fight, don't be afraid to fight dirty. For example, launching a bloody and excessive biting attack on one of the attackers can serve as a powerful sign of your violent intent. A swift kick to the groin can also quickly incapacitate one of your opponents and even the odds.

397. GET UP!

If you are on the floor surrounded by a group of attackers, punch and kick outward from the ground. Try to create a brief window in which you can get to your feet.

398. GAME CHANGER

Never underestimate the danger of a knife attack. Many of the conventional blocks and grappling techniques used in the martial arts can expose you to life-threatening injuries in a knife attack.

399. PROTECT VITAL POINTS

Have clear priorities when dealing with an attacker armed with a knife. Your first priority is to prevent your torso, throat, and face from being stabbed. You might have to accept cuts on less vulnerable parts of your body.

400. SHIELD DEFENSE

If confronted with a knife-wielding attacker, your first move should be to try to find some sort of protective shield. A thick backpack or bag will work as a shield. Other possibilities include books and magazines.

401. CLOTHING PROTECTION

If you get the chance, you can whip off a thick coat and wrap it around your front forearm, using this arm to deflect the knife blows.

402. KNIFE LETHALITY

At close ranges, a knife is more deadly than a gun. A knife inflicts a wound on both insertion and extraction, and it doesn't need reloading.

403. WRIST GRAB

A seemingly obvious objective is to try to control the attacker's knife hand by grabbing his wrist. However, be careful. The opponent might simply twist his wrist to escape, resulting in the knife's cutting into the arteries on your wrist.

404. WRIST CONTROL

If you do manage to control the knife hand, try to do so with both hands, twisting your torso around and away from the knife to reduce the risk to your vital organs.

405. RUBBER KNIFE DRILL

If you want to practice knife-fighting drills, use a rubber knife with the edge coated in red lipstick. Every "cut" will be revealed on your body with a red mark.

406. RANGE OF ATTACKS

Remember that the knife attacker isn't armed only with a knife. He can also punch and kick. Don't be completely focused on the knife. Be prepared to defend yourself against a full range of attacks.

407. X-BLOCK DANGER

Don't block a knife thrust with an X-block or any sort of forearm block. This will leave you exposed to wrist cuts, and it also opens up your torso to a fast stabbing counterstrike.

408. SIMULTANEOUS ATTACK

The critical objective in a defense against a knife attack is to counter the knife thrusts and to make a simultaneous attack. Don't leave a gap between your defense and offense, because a gap is an opportunity for the attacker to strike again.

409. SERIOUS COUNTERS

Be fierce when making any attacks against an opponent armed with a knife. Go for the throat and eyes, or aim for a fight-stopping knockout punch. Do something that will seriously injure the assailant.

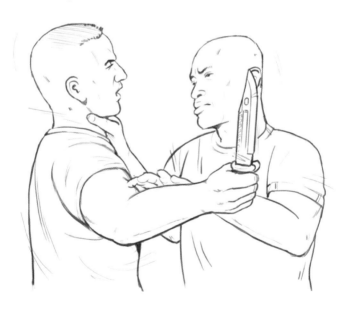

410. KEEP YOUR DISTANCE

Never be tempted to get in close and slug it out with an opponent armed with a knife. Make and keep your distance. Footwork can be the key to your survival.

411. STABBING ACTION

If the attacker chops at you with a downward stabbing action, strike his knife hand with your forearm, bent at the elbow at a 90-degree angle to keep the knife away from your upper chest and face.

412. DEFLECTION AND STRIKE

At the same time that you apply the forearm deflection, drive your fist into your opponent's throat or face. Follow up with fast repeated blows. Don't let the attacker recover his ground.

413. KNIFE GRAB

With some training, you can disarm an attacker if you can control his knife-hand forearm. Using your free hand, push his knife hand back to the wrist, and then unfold the wrist again, clawing the knife from his grip as you do so.

414. CONTROL THE MOVEMENT

If you deflect the knife hand but the opponent still makes a stabbing motion, quickly move forward, pushing against his arm to limit the range of movement he can use.

415. OUT OF LINE

When deflecting a knife attack, also move your torso out of the line of the knife's thrust. Try to open up angles of attack for punching counterstrikes.

416. KNIFE TO THROAT 1

If an attacker grabs you from behind, with a knife to your throat, first move your torso backward so your body is as close to his as possible.

417. KNIFE TO THROAT 2

If the attacker is holding the knife with his right hand, press your right elbow against the outside of his right elbow. Insert the fingers of your left hand on the inside of the knife-hand forearm. You can now push the knife arm away from your throat.

418. KNIFE TO THROAT 3

Now move your hands from right to left like the motion of car wiper blades, pushing the knife away from your throat and straightening out your opponent's knife arm.

419. KNIFE TO THROAT 4

Quickly turn to face your opponent, keeping full control of the knife arm and twisting it back over his right shoulder to deliver a compliance maneuver.

420. ARMED RESPONSE

The best defense against a knife is to have a weapon that you can use in response. A heavy club or baseball bat is ideal for hitting your opponent outside the range of his knife, or for breaking his wrist or arm before he can make an attack.

421. DEFLECTIONS

Note that we use the word "deflection" and not "block" to talk about countering the knife. Never use a single static block to stop a knife. A deflection implies an ultra-quick retraction to prevent your arm from being cut while at the same time parrying away the knife.

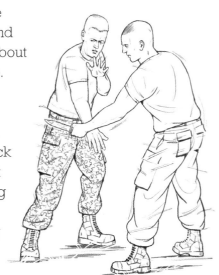

422. MAKE A SMALL TARGET

If threatened with a knife, make yourself as awkward a target as possible. Angle your torso at 45 degrees to your opponent, and use your leading arm to cover the side of your rib cage and abdomen, while your rear arm protects the front of your chest and stomach.

423. MAKE A HARD TARGET

Above all, keep moving during a knife encounter. The attacker is looking for a clear target, and is likely to advance straight at you, so keep side-stepping his advance. A kick to your attacker's shin can help create space.

424. DYNAMIC ACTION

Remember that a knife attack is dynamic. Many demonstrations show a choreographed routine with a single technique against a compliant training partner. In reality, the knife attacker will be continually stabbing and slashing.

425. ATTACK TO THE BLIND SIDE

A knife attacker can be focused on his weapon, forgetting about an all-around defense. Look for an exposed jaw to make a quick knockout blow.

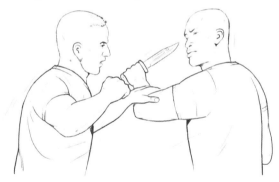

426. WIDER TARGETS

Remember that your arms are also secondary targets. Don't leave them exposed to quick slashing attacks—keep moving them to avoid giving your opponent a static target.

427. FIREARM TYPES

To defend against gunfire, you need to understand the different capabilities of each type of firearm, particularly in terms of range penetration.

428. HANDGUNS

Handguns have a limited effective range of about 150 feet, although a handgun bullet can be lethal at ranges of more than 300 feet. Most handgun bullets are stopped by light material surfaces, such as walls and car bodies.

429. SUBMACHINE GUNS

Submachine guns fire pistol-caliber ammunition, but their longer barrels give them a better range than handguns—more than 500 feet. What makes them truly dangerous is their full-auto fire capability.

430. RIFLES

Rifles, whether bolt-action, semiautomatic, or full-auto, have a long range. It is sometimes in excess of 3,000 feet. Depending on the ammunition type, rifle bullets can penetrate through heavy cover, including walls, sheet metal, and even some types of body armor.

431. SHOTGUNS

Shotguns have a similar range to handguns, but they are far more dangerous at close ranges because of the wounding effects delivered by the multiple shot pellets. However, such pellets tend to have very limited penetration.

432. HIGH-RISK SETTINGS

In a self-defense situation, you are unlikely to encounter an enemy armed with a machine gun, but in high-risk countries this is a possibility. A machine gun fires rifle-caliber ammunition and is fully automatic over long ranges. It can cut apart heavy cover.

433. COVER AND CONCEALMENT

To defend against firearms, you have to understand the difference between cover and concealment. Not making the distinction can be a life-threatening mistake in a shootout.

434. COVER

Cover is any object or structure that visually shields you from the shooter but does not provide significant protection against the bullets. Good examples of this include light vegetation and thin plasterboard walls.

435. CONCEALMENT

Concealment is any object or structure that not only hides you from view, but which also protects against any oncoming fire. Examples include earthen banks, steel girders, thick walls, and automobile engines.

436. IDENTIFYING COVER

In any shootout situation, make obtaining cover
your priority. Don't move from one position until
you clearly identify the next point of cover. Take
rapid glances around your existing point of cover
to identify the next position, but don't expose your
head for more than a fraction of a second.

437. SELECTING COVER

If you're under fire from someone armed with a
powerful rifle, carefully think about the type of cover
you adopt. Hiding behind a car door will offer little
protection from the bullets, but squatting behind the
engine block will provide excellent cover.

438. DEGRADED COVER

Remember that cover can be steadily degraded by continual bullet impacts, particularly from a powerful weapon such as a rifle or machine gun. If your position has been identified and is being struck by repeated fire, it is advisable to move to another piece of cover if it is safe to do so.

439. TIMING MOVEMENT

When sprinting between pieces of cover, don't be exposed for too long. You can use the following military mantra to get the timing right: "I'm up, I'm moving, he's seen me, DOWN!" If you say this command out loud, and literally obey its timing, the shooter won't have enough time to aim and fire a shot at you.

440. INACCURATE WEAPONS

The most common weapon used in armed assaults is the handgun. Although handguns are portable and easily concealed, they are very inaccurate, especially at longer ranges.

441. INEXPERIENCED SHOOTER

The way someone points a handgun at you will tell you a lot about his expertise with the weapon. A one-handed grip, especially with the weapon presented at an unusual angle, indicates that the shooter is not experienced with using a handgun.

442. TWO-HANDED GRIP

If the gunman holds the handgun with a stable two-handed grip, his legs shoulder-width apart, and his body facing you or standing at a 45-degree angle, then he's probably proficient in handling the weapon.

443. GUN SNATCH

It is possible to snatch a handgun from an assailant, although the move needs to be very fast and delivered with total confidence and fluidity. If the shooter is holding the gun in his right hand, strike the gun barrel to your right with your left hand, while simultaneously slapping the opponent's wrist to your left with your right hand. If the technique is good, the gun might fly right out of his hand.

444. QUICK RESPONSE

If your opponent pulls a handgun on you at close range, and if you have time, you can try to grab the gun hand with both hands to control its direction. In this situation, a gun can accidentally fire. Try to force his hands so the gun barrel points away from you. If possible, use powerful elbow jabs to the face to disorient him.

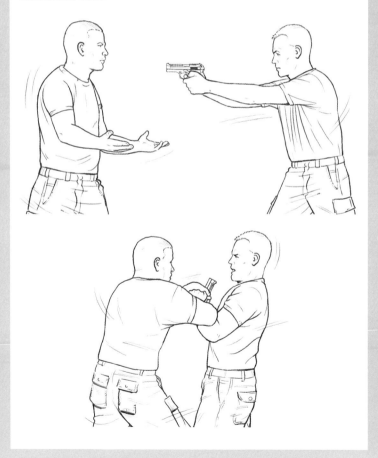

445. DISARMING

If the disarming is performed in a fast and hard manner, the gun can be knocked from your opponent's hand. You might be able to grab the gun.

446. LINE OF FIRE

When parrying or grabbing a gun, slip your body and head away from the direction of the gun, in case it accidentally goes off during the defensive move.

447. MOMENT TO STRIKE

The best point at which to grab a gunman's weapon is when he is talking and gesticulating. This is because his mind is temporarily disengaged from the thought of pulling the trigger.

448. COMPLIANCE

Attempt the gun grab only if you are very confident that you can move fast enough to do it. If the gun is being used to coerce you into giving money, just hand over your wallet immediately.

449. BEND BACK

The trick is to bend the gun right back toward the shooter's body, extending the angle of the gun beyond the limits of the shooter's wrist bend. You can accent the gun grab with an additional attack, such as a powerful hook punch to the jawline.

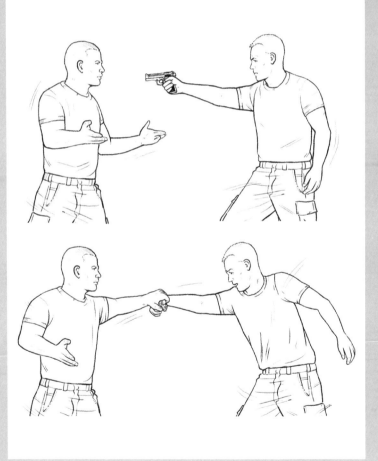

450. REVOLVER CONTROL

If you grab a revolver in the shooter's hand, try to get hold of the revolver cylinder to prevent it from turning when the shooter pulls the trigger. If the hammer of the gun is visibly cocked, however, the gun will be able to fire without the rotation of the cylinder, just a light pull on the trigger.

451. NUMBER OF SHOTS

If someone is shooting at you, and you have identified the type of weapon, count the number of shots and listen for the pause when the shooter has to reload. A handgun magazine will typically hold up to 13 or 14 rounds, a revolver takes up to six rounds, an assault rifle has up to 35, and a submachine gun has 35 to 50.

452. RELOAD DANGER

If the shooter stops to reload, use that moment to move between positions of cover, to make your escape, or to go on the attack—but be careful. An experienced gunman will take only a few seconds to reload, especially if he has spare magazines at the ready in ammo holsters.

453. LAST POINT OF COVER

When moving from cover to cover, try to leave your cover using a different angle or position from the one you took when you entered it. This is because the gunman is likely to have his weapon trained on the point at which he last saw you, waiting for you to emerge. Move to the side or back, staying out of sight before sprinting into the open.

454. LOW PROFILE

When you are moving about in a shooting situation, keep a very low profile, making sure your head is well down below the tops of walls. Never allow your silhouette to show against the skyline.

455. EVASIVE MANEUVERS

If you're fleeing from gunfire, quickly run in a
straight line between proximate pieces of cover, to
limit your time exposed to fire. If you're in the open,
with some distance between cover, occasionally
make some evasive turns to throw off the gunner's
aim, although not so many to slow you down.

456. LINE OF FIRE

Remember that firearms are "line-of-sight"
weapons, meaning that the shooter generally needs
to see you to hit you.
Your first priority for
survival, therefore,
is to use objects
and positions
of cover to break
visual contact.

457. SCATTER

A shooter in a public place will, unfortunately, be presented with a mass of possible targets. Basic military training can help you here. The shooter will more likely fire at a concentrated group of people, rather than an isolated individual, so scatter, and don't be tempted to cluster together with others.

458. SELF-PROTECTION

If police or counterterrorist forces engage the shooter, be very careful, as the rescuers will often have little time to distinguish between friend and foe. If possible, stay low on the ground with your hands visible, and don't stand up or run unless absolutely necessary or if instructed to do so by the law-enforcement officers.

459. IMPROVISED ARMOR

Improvise body armor by sticking thick books, pieces of wood, and any other flat, solid objects down your shirt or jacket. They might not stop the bullet entirely, but they will certainly deplete some of its energy.

460. SURVIVAL INSTINCT

If a shooter has himself been shot by police, continue to regard him as dangerous until you know otherwise. An energized gunner can remain a threat for many minutes, even after being restrained or receiving a fatal wound.

461. OVERPENETRATION

Be aware that bullets often penetrate through light targets, and continue in flight at odd angles. Therefore, even if you are not the shooter's principal focus, put a lot of lateral distance between yourself and the target.

462. USE YOUR EARS

If you can't see the shooter, use your hearing to determine where the shots are coming from. Turn your head from side to side to improve your sense of auditory location.

463. DISARMING AN OPPONENT WITH A RIFLE

If held at the point of a rifle, and the gunman is momentarily distracted, rush inside the arc of the rifle, grab hold of the muzzle, and with the other hand make a takedown strike.

464. GUNSHOT WOUNDS

If you happen to be shot during an engagement, don't panic and automatically assume that the wound will be fatal. In fact, most gunshot wound victims survive their injuries.

465. POINTS OF FOCUS

If you're being shot at, avoid running toward places that will be natural focal points for the gunman, such as doors, large windows, or alleys.

466. KNOW THE BUILDING

When you check into a hotel or go into any public building, try to become familiar with the floor plan and layout. Know where you can find entrances and exits, and how you can enter non-public spaces such as kitchens and staff rooms.

467. FRAGILE SURFACES

Try to avoid standing near anything that will shatter or explode when you are under gunfire. Instead, stand near materials that will absorb bullets, such as earth and thick wood.

468. FIGHT BACK

Recognize the fact that you cannot always hide from a gunman. If you are cornered, grab the most effective weapon that you can find and prepare to go on a vicious attack.

469. EQUALIZER

An improvised weapon can be used as an equalizer if you're facing a more powerful opponent or multiple attackers. However, don't make your defense entirely reliant upon a weapon.

470. CLUB WEAPONS

The simplest improvised weapon is any object that can be used as a club, from wooden handles to steel pipes, or sporting equipment such as baseball bats.

471. HOLDING BACK

When handling a club, don't wave it in front of your body, as this provides an opportunity for your opponent to grab it from you. Keep it held back to give you maximum space to build up to an effective strike impact.

472. STICK THRUST

Longer sticks can be used as thrusting weapons, aiming for the face and the ribs. Point the stick directly toward your opponent's face, and then thrust it forward using the back hand, allowing the shaft of the stick to run through the looped fingers of the front hand.

473. LIGHT VS. HEAVY CLUBS

The weight of a club dictates the manner of its use. If it is long and heavy, opt for a two-handed grip; use a single-handed grip if the club is short and light.

474. CLUB TARGETS

When delivering a club attack, strike at targets such as the forearms, elbows, knees, and even the face and the top of the skull if the situation is serious enough.

475. PULL BACK

Immediately after making a strike with a club, quickly pull it back to prevent it from being grabbed. Use your free hand, if you have one, to maintain a guard to the front.

476. HAMMERFIST WEAPON

A very short piece of wood, or indeed any heavy object that can be held in the palm of the hand, can be used as a hammerfist striking weapon or to add more power to a conventional punch.

477. CLUB IMPACT

When delivering a strike with a club, use your full body weight to press home the blow, much as with a punch. Make a deep strike into your target, not just against the surface of the body.

478. SPEED OF SWING

Remember that the effect of the club is maximized by the speed of the swing. Position yourself so that you can deliver the strike in a fast, wide arc without getting the club caught on any surfaces or objects during its flight.

479. BLINDING AN ASSAILANT

There are several household objects that can be used to blind an opponent, at least temporarily. Good examples are tubs of talcum powder (especially the squeezable type), aerosol cans (hair spray, deodorant, and so on), and powdered makeup.

480. DISTRACTION TOOL

Remember, if you're holding an improvised weapon, this might be all that your opponent focuses upon. This distraction can leave you openings for other attacks, such as jabs, punches, or kicks, which in turn can give you openings to deploy the weapon.

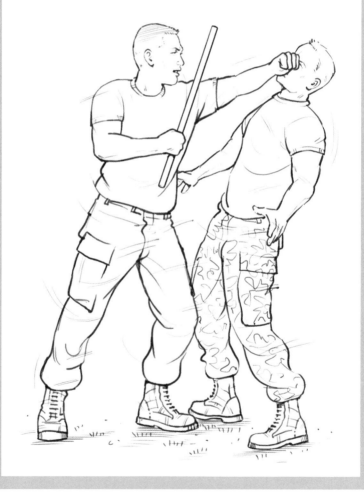

481. CAMERA LIGHT

Shine the camera light of your mobile phone directly into your opponent's eyes, holding the phone in your front hand. His natural tendency will be to smack away the light, which forces him to drop his guard, thus giving you an opportunity to deliver a powerful cross or hook punch.

482. COMMON OBJECTS

Among the most practical improvised weapons are objects you carry all the time, such as a bunch of keys or pens. Have them at the ready in an easily accessible pocket, not at the bottom of a deep bag.

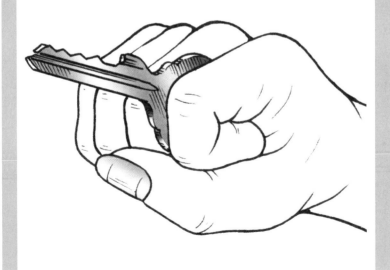

483. KNUCKLE DUSTER

You can arrange a bunch of keys into an improvised knuckle duster by inserting an individual key between each finger of one hand and gripping the center of the bunch in your palm.

484. STEEL-BARREL PEN

The best writing utensils to use as improvised weapons are pens with a steel barrel. Plastic pens or pencils are likely to shatter upon impact, exposing your hands to cuts.

485. STABBING ACTION

Hold the pen in the center of your fist, pointing downward, and deliver heavy stabbing strikes to your opponent's arms, upper torso, face, and eyes.

486. DEFENSIVE SHIELD

Don't think of improvised weapons just in terms of attack. Think of them in terms of defense. A solid backpack, for example, can be hooked over one arm and used as a form of shield to protect against fists and weapon attacks.

487. EVERYDAY LETHAL POTENTIAL

In everyday situations, the most common forms of improvised weapons are cutlery and glassware, or gardening tools. Be aware that the injuries these items can inflict can be very serious, so only use them as weapons of last resort.

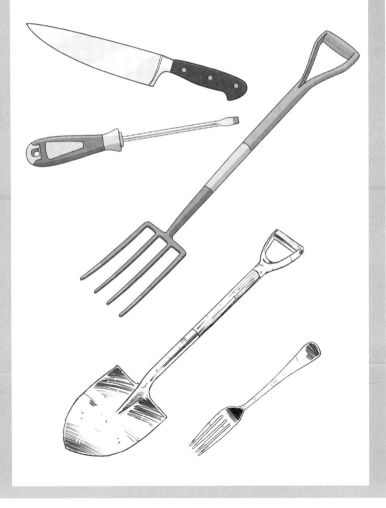

488. BE CREATIVE

Many apparently harmless-looking objects can
be turned into improvised weapons. Anything that
is handheld and heavy can be used as a striking
weapon. A pole or stick from a gardening implement
can make an excellent offensive device for jabbing.

489. HIDDEN WEAPONS

For home defense, it is a good idea to locate objects
that can be used as improvised weapons at various
points throughout the house. Keep them hidden from
open view and away from children.

490. THROWING WEAPONS

Throwing a handful of coins or a fistful of grit or dirt into your opponent's face will provide a few seconds of distraction and allow you to follow up with a more powerful attack. Heavier everyday objects can be thrown to deliver impact injuries in their own right.

491. CREDIT CARD SLASHER

Plastic credit cards can have surprisingly sharp edges. They can be used as slashing weapons. Make a firm scrape with the hard corner across your opponent's face, particularly aiming for the eyes.

492. RECOIL EFFECT

When using improvised weapons, be particularly aware of the issue of recoil. Think about the effect the weapon will have on your body as it recoils under the impact of the strike against your opponent.

493. ALUMINUM CAN BLADE

An aluminum can can be turned into a weapon in a matter of seconds. Empty the fluid and crush the can, an action that produces numerous sharp cutting edges.

494. FLUID DISTRACTION

If you are carrying a drink bottle, you can throw the contents into your opponent's face as a distraction. If the fluid is hot, the scalding effect can be enough to deter your opponent from attacking.

495. FIGHTING FLASHLIGHT

A large steel-framed flashlight is an excellent fighting device. Not only can the powerful beam be used to blind your opponent for a moment, but the flashlight body can be used as a heavy club or hammerfist weapon.

496. NEWSPAPER CLUB

Even a humble newspaper can be turned into an improvised weapon. Roll up several sections of a newspaper into a long shaft that can be held in your hand. Bend the shaft in half to form a substantial and convenient club for stabbing.

497. UMBRELLA SPEAR

You can use a steel-framed umbrella, especially one with a sharp tip, to make defensive blocks or stabbing attacks against your opponent's face and torso.

498. CHAIR PROTECTION

A chair that is light enough to pick up can be useful as a charging weapon. Run at your opponent with speed, driving the legs of the chair into or around his body and forcing him to move backward.

499. MAGAZINE JAB

A rolled-up magazine can deliver some extremely painful impact injuries if you jab the ends of the pages into the face or the soft areas of the throat.

500. ANTENNA WHIP

In a fight in a parking lot, you can snap off a car radio antenna and use it as a whip to make attacks against the face and the arms.

501. THINK CREATIVELY

The key to using improvised weapons is to think innovatively. Play a mental game in which you think up self-defense options for all the objects that you can see in the room around you. In an office scenario, a pen or pencil can make an excellent stabbing weapon.

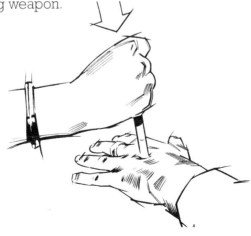

Index